"Looking for a primer on covenant theology that is grounded in biblical theology? This is your book. Crowe faithfully guides you from creation to the new creation through the nexus of God's covenant and human obedience."

Andrew T. Abernethy, associate professor of Old Testament at Wheaton College

"In *The Path of Faith*, Dr. Crowe clearly presents the various ways the law functions in redemptive history. He places the law in the context of the overarching covenantal structure of Scripture and shows how the requirement to perfectly keep the law of God continues today even after the failure of Adam, a requirement that is foundational to the gospel and fulfilled in Christ. This work also shows how the law functions in each of the Old Testament covenants, being fulfilled in the New Covenant, but also relevant for us today to experience the blessed life in God's kingdom. I highly recommend this book as a helpful guide to answer fundamental questions about the relationship between covenant, law, faith, and obedience."

Richard P. Belcher Jr., Gwin Professor of Old Testament and academic dean at Reformed Theological Seminary

"Dr. Crowe has written an accessible and insightful book, offering his view of some of the complex biblical and theological issues of the Christian's relationship to covenant, law, obedience, and life. Readers will not agree with everything in this book, yet Crowe's pastoral, biblical, and theological arguments can help Christians better understand 'the path of faith' for those in Christ. Dr. Crowe argues with force and clarity that those in Christ must obey God."

Jarvis J. Williams, associate professor of New Testament interpretation at The Southern Baptist Theological Seminary

"Much thanks to Dr. Crowe for giving us a penetrating and practical exploration of faith, covenant, and law as they develop throughout the Scriptures. His attention to every major portion of biblical history will help all followers of Christ discern how their Christian faith is inextricably rooted in the entire Bible."

Richard L. Pratt Jr., president, Third Millennium Ministries

THE PATH OF FAITH
A Biblical Theology
of Covenant and Law

BRANDON D. CROWE

An imprint of InterVarsity Press
Downers Grove, Illinois

InterVarsity Press
P.O. Box 1400, Downers Grove, IL 60515-1426
ivpress.com
email@ivpress.com

*InterVarsity Press® is the book-publishing division of InterVarsity Christian Fellowship/USA®, a movement
of students and faculty active on campus at hundreds of universities, colleges, and schools of nursing
in the United States of America, and a member movement of the International Fellowship of Evangelical Students.
For information about local and regional activities, visit intervarsity.org.*

Cover design and image composite: David Fassett
Interior design: Daniel van Loon
Image: geometric pattern: © ExpressIPhoto / iStock / Getty Images Plus

ISBN 978-0-8308-5537-7 (print)
ISBN 978-0-8308-5538-4 (digital)

Printed in the United States of America ♾

*InterVarsity Press is committed to ecological stewardship and to the conservation of natural resources
in all our operations. This book was printed using sustainably sourced paper.*

Library of Congress Cataloging-in-Publication Data
A catalog record for this book is available from the Library of Congress.

P 25 24 23 22 21 20 19 18 17 16 15 14 13 12 11 10 9 8 7 6 5 4 3 2

Y 39 38 37 36 35 34 33 32 31 30 29 28 27 26 25 24 23 22

For Eliza Cate

CONTENTS

SERIES PREFACE

BENJAMIN L. GLADD

THE ESSENTIAL STUDIES IN BIBLICAL THEOLOGY is patterned after the highly esteemed series New Studies in Biblical Theology, edited by D. A. Carson. Like the NSBT, this series is devoted to unpacking the various strands of biblical theology. The field of biblical theology has grown exponentially in recent years, showing no sign of abating. At the heart of biblical theology is the unfolding nature of God's plan of redemption as set forth in the Bible.

With an influx of so many books on biblical theology, why generate yet another series? A few reasons. The ESBT is dedicated to the fundamental or "essential" broad themes of the grand story line of the Bible. Stated succinctly, the goal of the ESBT series is to explore the *central* biblical-theological themes of the Bible. Several existing series on biblical theology are generally open-ended, whereas the ESBT will be limited to ten or so volumes. By restricting the entire series, the scope of the project is established from the beginning. The ESBT project functions as a whole in that each theme is intentional, and each volume does not stand solely on its own merits. The individual volumes interlock with one another and, taken together, form a complete and cohesive unit.

Another unique dimension of the series is a robust emphasis on biblical theology, spanning the entire sweep of the history of redemption. Each volume traces a particular theme throughout the Bible, from Genesis 1–3 to Revelation 21–22, and is organically connected to the person of Christ and the church in the New Testament. To avoid a "flat" biblical theology, these projects are mindful of how the New Testament develops their topic in fresh or unexpected ways. For example, the New Testament sheds new light on the nature of the "kingdom" and "messiah." Though these twin themes are rooted and explored in the Old Testament, both flow through the person of Christ in unique ways. Biblical theology should include how Old Testament themes are held in continuity and discontinuity with the New Testament.

The audience of the series includes beginning students of theology, church leaders, and laypeople. The ESBT is intended to be an accessible introduction to core biblical-theological themes of the Bible. This series is not designed to overturn every biblical-theological rock and investigate the finer details of biblical passages. Each volume is intentionally brief, serving as a primer of sorts that introduces the reader to a particular theme. These works also attempt to apply their respective biblical-theological themes to Christian living, ministry, and worldview. Good biblical theology warms the heart and motivates us to grow in our knowledge and adoration of the triune God.

AUTHOR'S PREFACE

THE TOPICS COVERED IN THIS BOOK are some of the most important for understanding the contents of the Bible and how we live on a daily basis. Covenant and law in Scripture are vast topics that have garnered a great deal of discussion. My goal is to show the unity of the biblical witness and the consistent call for God's people to covenant loyalty, all while recognizing the unique, saving work of Christ on our behalf. Each chapter includes discussion of biblical texts, practical application, and suggestions for further reading. Consistent with the aim of the ESBT series, this book covers Genesis 1 to Revelation 22 in order, providing a sense of the scope and development of the themes of covenant and law. I have tried to keep technical language and footnotes to a minimum, but sometimes footnotes have been necessary, especially where I am indebted to the insights of others.

An important caveat is necessary here at the outset. Addressing covenant and law means addressing the overarching structure of Scripture. This involves a number of interrelated theological commitments and presuppositions that I do not have space to defend here—such as the nature of Scripture (its inspiration, authority, clarity, unity, and so forth), the doctrine of God, the person and work of Christ, the unity of the human race, and so forth. Though the scope of the project does not allow a full discussion of these commitments, their importance will be necessary for the arguments and conclusions that follow. Pulling the string in one area will affect others as well. Put differently, covenant and law are not isolated issues but relate to a range of other doctrines and fit within one's overall hermeneutical approach to Scripture. I hope that what I write will be beneficial to a wide audience, even though those with different perspectives might frame things differently.

In addition, what follows is in many ways a *synthesis* written in an accessible, nontechnical manner. Because of this, I have not typically considered alternative interpretations. To do so would be worthwhile but would result in a different sort of book (a much longer one). While I will consider the details of many texts in what follows, this book often represents the *fruit* of close exegesis one can find explained and defended in more technical ways elsewhere. This is also a work of *biblical theology*, which means I consider each passage in light of the canon as a whole. This approach explains why I sometimes cite works of systematic theology. Such works often provide some of the most detailed, thorough discussions of exegetical questions. Additionally, systematic theology considers the scope of all Scripture. It is therefore quite helpful when addressing issues of whole-Bible biblical theology. I also find an absolute dichotomization between biblical and systematic theology to be anachronistic and unworkable in practice. For at every turn we must make theological conclusions from Scripture. Why not do so by listening to those who have engaged the exegetical questions at great length?

For the topics of covenant and law I am particularly indebted to the comprehensive works of Francis Turretin and Herman Bavinck. These have shaped my thinking in many ways, and I readily acknowledge my debt, but I have cited them as sparingly as possible, typically only where I follow their particular ways of framing a point. Even so, the framework for the following discussion is not the property of one or two interpreters; it is strongly established more broadly in the Reformed theological tradition from which I write. While new questions arise and old debates persist, the basic framework—which I find to be the most faithful to the biblical texts—has endured for hundreds of years. I have therefore sought to provide a modern-day, distinctive presentation of issues that I am not the first to address. I hope to present in a new way this unified understanding of Scripture, through the lens of covenant and law, highlighting both the glorious work of Christ on our behalf and our continued call to glorify God with lives of obedience.

Thanks to Ben Gladd for the opportunity to contribute to the ESBT series. I resonate with the goal of the series and welcome the opportunity to help make biblical theology widely accessible. It has also been my pleasure to work with Anna Gissing and the fine team at InterVarsity Press—a publisher with a long tradition of excellence.

Thanks to the faculty and Board of Trustees of Westminster Theological Seminary for granting a Professional Advancement Leave in the first half of 2019, which provided me the opportunity to write the bulk of this manuscript. I was sharpened and instructed by conversations about this book with numerous conversation partners, particularly my colleagues at Westminster Theological Seminary. Thanks especially to Dick Belcher, Bob Cara, Jennifer Chun, Stephen Coleman, Bill Fullilove, and Vern Poythress, all of whom commented on written portions of the manuscript.

I am profoundly grateful for the love and support of my family, especially my wife Cheryl. I dedicate this volume with love to my daughter, Eliza Cate. She is a true delight—a joyous reminder of what life is designed to be like in the context of the covenant.

ABBREVIATIONS

AJEC   Ancient Judaism and Early Christianity
BECNT   Baker Exegetical Commentary on the New Testament
BZNW   Beihefte zur Zeitschrift für die neutestamentliche
            Wissenschaft
CAHQ   Christian Answers to Hard Questions
CBQ   *Catholic Biblical Quarterly*
CCT   Contours of Christian Theology
EEC   Evangelical Exegetical Commentary
ESBT   Essential Studies in Biblical Theology
ICC   International Critical Commentary
Inst.   Turretin, Francis. *Institutes of Elenctic Theology*. Edited by
            James T. Dennison Jr. Translated by George Musgrave
            Giger. 3 vols. Phillipsburg, NJ: P&R, 1992–97.
JSNTSup   Journal for the Study of the New Testament Supplement Series
LCC   Library of Christian Classics
NAC   New American Commentary
NACSBT   New American Commentary Studies in Bible and Theology
NICNT   New International Commentary on the New Testament

NICOT	New International Commentary on the Old Testament
NIGTC	New International Greek Testament Commentary
NIVAC	NIV Application Commentary
NSBT	New Studies in Biblical Theology
NTC	New Testament Commentary
NTR	New Testament Readings
OTL	Old Testament Library
PNTC	Pelican New Testament Commentary
RD	Bavinck, Herman. *Reformed Dogmatics*. Edited by John Bolt. Translated by John Vriend. 4 vols. Grand Rapids, MI: Baker Academic, 2003–8.
SNTSMS	Society for New Testament Studies Monograph Series
SSBT	Short Studies in Biblical Theology
SSEJC	Studies in Scripture in Early Judaism and Christianity
TNTC	Tyndale New Testament Commentary
TOTC	Tyndale Old Testament Commentary
VTSup	Supplements to Vetus Testamentum
WBC	Word Biblical Commentary
WCF	Westminster Confession of Faith
WLC	Westminster Larger Catechism
WTJ	*Westminster Theological Journal*

INTRODUCTION

TIME WAS SHORT. THE STAKES WERE HIGH. He had to get moving. Yet the path was lined with peril in every direction. Many had fallen before him. But he had a major advantage that others did not have—a book from his father that showed him the way. It wouldn't be easy, but he had a sense of what to expect. He had to walk by faith. Before him stood the goal of eternal life and the chance to save others based on his actions.

That man was renowned archaeologist Dr. Henry Jones Jr.—better known as Indiana. He faced three lethal challenges to reach the legendary cup of Christ that provided life and healing for his father, who had received a mortal wound.

Those events from *Indiana Jones and the Last Crusade* are fictitious. There is no canyon of the crescent moon that leads to a temple, which is home to an ancient knight who guards a magical cup of Christ.[1] But it does illustrate several elements that I will address in this book. The Bible speaks of a problem that brings death; there is also a path that leads to life—one that we walk by faith—and we have an inspired book that explains it. And in that book we

---

[1] Though the ancient city of Petra, where the external scenes of the supposed ancient temple were filmed, is quite real.

meet the one who walked the path before us, in order to save us from the sting of death. I'll even discuss the cup of Christ from the last supper, though the New Testament writers construe it quite differently from the movie. The cup itself holds no supernatural powers, but it does indeed point the way to eternal life.

In what follows, I trace the themes of *covenant* and *law* in Scripture. These are two of the most important topics in Scripture, and they are closely related. They address how God voluntarily condescends to relate to us and how we ought to live on a daily basis. We must remember that the Bible is not at its core a book of abstract philosophy but is given to guide us in what we are to believe and how we ought to live. In this book I hope you will see how practical these issues are.

The topics of covenant and law are complex and have often been debated, but I'm not interested in getting bogged down in technical debates. Instead, in this book I make four key points.

1. All people are obligated to obey their Creator.
2. Though he did not have to, from the beginning God freely entered into a covenant with humanity to offer a reward upon the condition of perfect obedience.
3. Only Jesus perfectly obeys God's law, which is necessary for eternal life. Eternal life is granted by grace through faith on the basis of Christ's work.
4. Even though we can't perfectly obey God's law, the law continues to guide us in how we should live. Obedience to God's law is still required. And yet obedience is not a burden but the path of blessing.

These are four landmarks to maintain your bearings in the discussion that follows, and they also serve as a handy summary of the book. But to use these terms raises some immediate questions. What is a covenant? What is the law? Why are these important? Such terms must be clearly defined.

DEFINING KEY TERMS

Covenant. Let's start with *covenant.* Though this term can be used in a variety of ways in common speech (e.g., "the covenant of marriage"), *covenant* is also a technical term used quite a bit in theology. Some theological systems are even described using this term, such as "covenant theology" or "progressive covenantalism." These descriptors pick up on the Bible's use of *covenant*, which is an important term in both the Old and New Testaments.

As with many important theological terms, some debate exists regarding how best to define a covenant. But at its core, a covenant is a binding arrangement—a contract of sorts—between two or more parties. Sometimes in the ancient world these parties were equals, but often one party was more powerful than the other. In such situations, a lesser king (or nation) was obligated to show loyalty to a greater king in light of the benefits bestowed by that greater king. Where loyalty is maintained, blessings will accrue to the lesser nation. But where the treaty is transgressed, punishment will follow. These particular types of covenants, memorably named "suzerain vassal treaties,"[2] were common in the ancient Near East (the cultural context of the ancient Israelites), and help us understand portions of the Old Testament.

Ancient treaties such as these can provide helpful cultural context for understanding Scripture's emphasis on covenants, especially in the Old Testament. At the same time, biblical covenants are not exactly like ancient Near Eastern, nonbiblical covenants. *Biblical covenants can be defined as elected (as opposed to natural) relationships of obligation, typically ratified by an oath, that include blessings for obedience and curses for disobedience.*[3] Throughout Scripture people and nations make covenants with other people or nations.[4] These covenants between people(s) are important, but I will focus specifically on covenants between God and humanity. These include covenants with Adam, Noah, Abraham, Moses, and David; and the new covenant. Though diverse, these covenants also share some key features, as we will see throughout this study.

---

[2]For a brief overview of such treaties, see Brandon D. Crowe, *The Obedient Son: Deuteronomy and Christology in the Gospel of Matthew*, BZNW 188 (Berlin: de Gruyter, 2012), 90-95.

[3]This is a modification of the definition used in Crowe, *Obedient Son*, 91. It derives from Gordon Paul Hugenberger, *Marriage as Covenant: A Study of Biblical Law and Ethics Governing Marriage Developed from the Perspective of Malachi*, VTSup 52 (Leiden: Brill, 1994), 171; see also Dennis E. Johnson, *Walking with Jesus Through His Word: Discovering Christ in All the Scriptures* (Phillipsburg, NJ: P&R, 2015), 90-95.

[4]See, for example, Abraham and Abimelech (Gen 21:27), Jacob and Laban (Gen 31:44), the Israelites and the Gibeonites (Josh 9:15).

Besides these specific covenants made in Scripture, there is also another way to organize the teaching of Scripture using covenants. Some theological traditions have organized all of God's dealings with humanity under the headings of two overarching covenants: the covenant of works and the covenant of grace. The covenant of works was made with Adam and continues to be the operative principle for all who are "in Adam" (that is, all those who do not believe in Christ). The covenant of grace refers to God's gracious plan of redemption and applies to all of those "in Christ" (see Rom 5:12-21). This includes anyone with true faith in God's promises—whether in the Old Testament era or New Testament era.

But these categories may introduce a range of new questions. Was Adam actually given a covenant? Does the term *works* imply Adam could earn a reward by his own efforts? Where do we find the covenant of grace in Scripture?

I will address these questions, especially in chapter one. I believe that organizing biblical covenants under the headings of two, overarching covenants (the covenant of works and the covenant of grace) is legitimate and helpful. I will mention these two overarching categories at points in this book, but they will not be the focus of the chapters that follow. Instead, they provide more of the substructure that underlies my discussion. Without understanding these overarching covenants, we risk misconstruing covenant and law, especially in the Old Testament. Even so, I will be guided mostly by the structure of specific covenants in biblical history.

Law. *Law* can be used quite broadly in Scripture. Law often refers to the law(s) of Moses in the Old Testament or to the section of the Bible known as the Pentateuch (also known as the Five Books of Moses or the Torah): Genesis, Exodus, Leviticus, Numbers, and Deuteronomy. At the same time, *law* elsewhere in Scripture can refer to the entire Old Testament, to the covenant of works (more on this later), the old covenant, or to what God requires of humanity.[5] In this latter sense the law is most fully (though not exclusively) set forth in the law of Moses. Even though many of the laws given through Moses were for a more limited purpose, the abiding requirements of God's moral law are set forth with particular clarity in the Pentateuch.

---

[5]Turretin, *Inst.* 11.1.3 (2:1).

RELATING COVENANT AND LAW

Now that we've seen some basic definitions of covenant and law, it will be helpful to address how they are related. Simply put, covenants entail obligations. Since the days of Adam, God has always interacted with humanity by means of covenants, and covenants have stipulations that require obedience. The covenant with Adam required perfect obedience, and subsequent covenants continue to require God's people to obey God's commands as they walk in fellowship with him.

We see something similar reflected in daily life. If we return to the example of the marriage covenant, we find a *relationship* that also has certain *rules* associated with it. If a man and woman are married and love each other, having certain rules in place is necessary to guard and promote that relationship. For example, one rule is that a married individual cannot be married to two people at the same time. This is consistent with the common vow taken at weddings to "forsake all others." On the one hand, such language might sound harsh or restrictive. But on the other hand, such a vow is liberating and reflects one's highest commitments. A vow to monogamy makes sense in light of the importance and uniqueness of the marriage relationship. Saying "no" to marrying someone else enables husbands and wives to say "yes" to one another. Healthy parameters pave the way for a unique and fruitful relationship. Were someone to try to apply the popular cliché "love has no boundaries" to a marriage, it would border on the absurd. For surely if married love means to forsake all others, that means there *must* be boundaries to guard the relationship. This is why the bride and groom make wedding vows, committing to erect boundaries around their covenantal bond. Love must have boundaries.

This can help us understand the big picture of what it means to live in a relationship with God (think *covenant*) that also features rules (think *law*). God's law shows us the boundaries that he has given to us and how we ought to love him. The law provides guardrails for the covenant relationship. But as with any human analogy, the marriage analogy is also imperfect. The covenant of marriage differs significantly from God's covenants with us. God is our Creator. And because God is our Creator, he has ultimate authority over us. As created beings, we are obligated to obey our Creator. This was true already in the beginning, even before the entrance of sin into the world. We have always been obligated to love and obey our Creator. Even where the contours of the biblical covenants may differ in some ways, the necessity for creatures to live in relationship with God, while loving and obeying him, never ceases. It's also important to recognize that covenants are not only obligations for people, but God obligates himself as well.

As is always the case for covenantal arrangements, obedience to God brings great blessing. This does not mean that we will always be materially prosperous or that everything will go well for us in this age. Often in Scripture the realization of the promises of blessing comes in the future. But in the biblical worldview, blessing is particularly tied to the blessing of God's covenant presence—the promise that he will be with us as our God. This is apparent in the covenant formula we find throughout Scripture, such as in Jeremiah 7:23: "Obey my voice, and I will be your God, and you shall be my people."[6] The repeated affirmation that God will be the God of his people sums up the covenant relationship and unifies the various covenants.[7] The blessings of the covenant are preeminently the blessings of God's presence, and the way we walk in his presence is by obedience to his commandments. Not only are the people obligated to walk in God's ways, but God himself enters into an obligation to bless his people. Further, since we are imperfect, the sacrificial system in the Old Testament, such as we find in Leviticus, is God's appointed means to enable the covenant fellowship that has been disrupted by our sin.[8] Both these elements point forward to Christ, who is Immanuel, the fulfillment of "God with us" (Mt 1:23; 18:20; 28:20), and is the final sacrifice for sin, enabling even greater fellowship with God (Heb 4:14-16).

Obeying God, in fellowship with him, is the path of faith—even where we are unable to obey God perfectly. At the same time, disobedience brings curse. Sin brings death and destruction, not life and prosperity. And yet Scripture teaches that God is gracious toward and patient with his people

---

[6]See also, e.g., Ex 6:6-7; 29:45; Jer 11:4; 30:22; Ezek 36:28.

[7]See O. Palmer Robertson, *The Christ of the Covenants* (Phillipsburg, NJ: P&R, 1980), 45-48; see also Richard P. Belcher Jr., *The Fulfillment of the Promises of God: An Explanation of Covenant Theology* (Fearn, Ross-shire: Mentor, 2020), 111, 111n51.

[8]See L. Michael Morales, *Who Shall Ascend the Mountain of the Lord? A Biblical Theology of the Book of Leviticus*, NSBT 37 (Downers Grove, IL: InterVarsity Press, 2015).

and does not treat them as they deserve. An important biblical text where we find this illustrated is Exodus 34:6-7:

> The LORD passed before him [Moses] and proclaimed, "The LORD, the LORD, a God merciful and gracious, slow to anger, and abounding in steadfast love and faithfulness, keeping steadfast love for thousands, forgiving iniquity and transgression and sin, but who will by no means clear the guilty, visiting the iniquity of the fathers on the children and the children's children, to the third and the fourth generation."

Our covenantal God is merciful. Even so, sin is a big problem that has to be addressed. God will by no means clear the guilty. Every person born naturally since Adam is a sinner. Since the entrance of sin into the world, no one can please God perfectly. Yet if we are to have a right standing before God, sin must somehow be overcome, disobedience punished, and entire righteousness realized. This will help us understand why it was necessary for Jesus to be perfectly obedient and to be the final sacrifice in the New Testament. I say all this by way of introduction; I will tease it out in much more detail in the chapters that follow.

OUTLINE

In this book I will look at God's covenants in Scripture sequentially, beginning with Genesis and ending in Revelation. The first five chapters deal with God's covenants in the Old Testament (Adam, Noah, Abraham, Moses, David), and the next five chapters address the new covenant. At the end of each chapter, I include points of application and suggestions for further reading.

My own tradition (Reformed theology), has quite a bit to say about covenants. Yet my aim is not simply to repeat traditional statements but to study the biblical texts themselves with an eye to how they relate to us today. For indeed, covenant and law are not only key concepts for understanding the coherence of the Scriptures; they are immensely practical topics that require a response from us. Therefore, we must give due diligence to considering how God continues to relate to us today.

Chapter One

THE BEGINNING

ADAM AND NOAH

WE WERE HALFWAY THROUGH THE MOVIE when the whispering started. It was difficult to tell what was happening a few seats down. Then someone passed the question to me: "How did he become Spiderman?"

My family and I had gone to view the anticipated movie *Spiderman 2*. Since this was a sequel, my mom, who had not seen the first movie, was in the dark. Sure, she could follow the story in general terms, but she wanted the backstory to understand all that was happening. It's not obvious how an ordinary teenager morphs into an arachnoid. That part is explained at the beginning of the first movie.

My mom's experience illustrates the importance the beginning of a story holds for making sense of things, which certainly applies to the Bible as well. If we want to understand the climax of the biblical story—which comes with Jesus in the New Testament—we must first understand the beginning. We need to understand how we get there. What were things like when the world was created? What was the goal? What should have happened? What went wrong? How did humanity go from a state of blessedness to a state of misery? How does this beginning anticipate the work of Christ thousands of years later? To answer such questions, we need to consider carefully what is said about Adam and Eve. We need to start at the beginning.

CONTEXT FOR COVENANT:
CREATOR RELATING TO CREATURE

The Bible begins with creation. More accurately, the Bible begins with *God* creating the heavens and the earth (Gen 1:1). We must recognize an important distinction from the outset: God is the Creator; everything else is created. This is often referred to as the Creator-creature distinction. Only God is self-existent. God does not need his creation. He does not owe his creatures anything. He is not in our debt. As created beings, all people are dependent on God for life and breath and everything (Acts 17:25). All people are created in the image of God and owe him obedience, for he has authority over us. From the time of Adam, God has related to people by means of *covenant*—thereby offering rewards for obedience, while also threatening curses for disobedience.

Parents of small children may strive to exhibit a high level of competence and social decorum in the professional world. But when they play with their children, parents will often get on the floor and roll around. They don't speak the language of the office; they speak in ways that their children can understand. They use words like peek-a-boo, blankie, and dolly to relate to, enjoy, and teach their children. Yet parents will also have rules for their children in order to help them thrive and succeed. A child may not be allowed to play next to a busy street. This is not because parents want to rob their children of joy, but because the traffic is dangerous and allowing a small child to play next to the street does not promote a full, blessed life. Children must trust that their parents have their best interests in mind.

This imperfect analogy reflects how God interacts with us. He relates to us and speaks in ways we can understand. His covenantal rules have our best interests in mind. This is an extremely practical point. A study of God's covenants should address how we relate to and live in fellowship with God each day.[1] And as we will see, obedience to God and fullness of life in the context of the covenant always go together.

ADAM AND THE COVENANT OF WORKS

Covenant with Adam. I mentioned above that the first covenant in the Bible was made with Adam. Yet this is a contested point. It has often been debated whether God actually enters into a covenant with Adam. For example, the term *covenant* (Hebrew: *bərît*) is not used for God's interactions with Adam in Genesis. But that's not all there is to say.

The best reading of Genesis 1–3, in the context of all of Scripture, is that God enters into a covenant with Adam. Before we can talk about the law given to Adam, we need to see several reasons why the term *covenant* is appropriate to describe God's interactions with Adam before sin entered the world.[2]

1. Elsewhere in Scripture God enters into special relationships with key people by means of covenants. Examples include covenants with Noah, Abraham, and David. Likewise, in Genesis 2:15-17 God enters into a special relationship with a key person—Adam. Though the term "covenant" is not used here, the concept is present.

2. Covenants have stipulations—things that must be done or avoided. Adam is required to love and obey God fully. In Genesis 1:28 Adam (along with Eve) is commanded to be fruitful and multiply and govern the world as God's image bearer. In Genesis 2:15 Adam is placed in the Garden of Eden to work in and guard it. Further, he is encouraged to eat from any tree in the Garden but is expressly prohibited from eating from one tree—the tree of the knowledge of good and evil (Gen 2:17). This specific test sums up all that is required of Adam, denoting the presence of covenantal stipulations.[3]

3. Covenants have consequences, depending on whether one obeys the covenant stipulations. These take the form of rewards (blessings) or

---

[1]See Geerhardus Vos, *Biblical Theology: Old and New Testaments* (1948; repr., Edinburgh: Banner of Truth, 1975), 8-9.
[2]Following especially Turretin, *Inst.* 8.3 (1:574-78).
[3]Louis Berkhof, *Systematic Theology*, 4th ed. (Grand Rapids, MI: Eerdmans, 1996), 216-17.

punishments (curses). In Genesis 2:17 death is threatened for disobedience. The positive side of this, which is implied by the text, is that a
greater experience of life would have been the reward for Adam's covenantal obedience. If Adam did not sin, he would not have died.
Instead, he would have experienced the increasing fullness of life
represented by the tree of life, which bestowed life sacramentally (see
Gen 3:22).[4] Adam would have been fruitful and multiplied, and
expanded God's dominion throughout the earth as God's vice-regent.[5]

4. Though the term *covenant* is not used in Genesis, Hosea 6:7 most likely
   does refer to a covenant with Adam: "But like Adam they transgressed
   the covenant; there they dealt faithlessly with me." Hosea likens the
   faithlessness of God's people in his day, who had violated the covenant,
   to Adam's violation of the covenant in the beginning.[6]

5. The way that the New Testament treats the work of Jesus in relation
   to Adam (e.g., Rom 5:12-21) makes the most sense if both Adam and
   Christ are covenant representatives, whose actions count for others.
   Just as Adam's actions brought death to all humanity "in Adam," so
   Christ's actions bring life to all those "in him." I'll address this point
   further in chapters five through ten.

Covenant of works? If there was a covenant with Adam, what were the
dynamics of that covenant? The focus of this book is on the relationship of
law and covenant. We therefore need to look in more detail at both the stipulations and the consequences for Adam, since these have implications for
what follows in the Bible.

---

[4]For these two points, see Turretin, *Inst.* 8.3.7 (1:575–76); Vos, *Biblical Theology*, 27–29.
[5]See further G. K. Beale, *A New Testament Biblical Theology: The Unfolding of the Old Testament in the New* (Grand Rapids, MI: Baker Academic, 2011), 32–46.
[6]Some suggest that Hos 6:7 refers to the *place* Adam (see also Josh 3:16, NIV, NRSV). That is pos-
sible but seems to require taking the Hebrew preposition *kaph* in *kə'ādām* in a rarer, locative
sense (or to emend the text to read *beth*), whereas *kaph*, the better reading, is more often taken
comparatively. Either way, a covenant of works is not dependent on one's rendering of Hosea 6:7.
I discuss these details further in *The Last Adam: A Theology of the Obedient Life of Jesus in the
Gospels* (Grand Rapids, MI: Baker Academic, 2017), 57-61; see also Richard P. Belcher Jr., "The
Covenant of Works in the Old Testament," in *Covenant Theology: Biblical, Theological, and Historical
Perspectives*, ed. Guy Prentiss Waters, J. Nicholas Reid, and John R. Muether (Wheaton, IL: Cross-
way, 2020), 63-78.

The covenant with Adam has various names, such as the covenant of life, the covenant of nature, the covenant of creation, and (most commonly) the covenant of works. Bringing the above observations together: the covenant of works teaches that Adam was created by God upright (see Eccles 7:29) but not yet possessing the fullness of eternal life. God condescended to Adam and entered into a covenant, and Adam was obligated to love and obey God fully. Adam was also given a specific test: he was prohibited from eating of the tree of the knowledge of good and evil. If Adam passed the test, God promised to grant him eternal life. If Adam sinned, he would die (Gen 2:17).

I believe this is the most biblical way to understand God's interactions with Adam in Genesis 1–3. Yet the terminology "covenant of works" is often questioned. To many, this sounds dangerously close to saying that Adam was supposed to *work* his way to God—that is, *earn* eternal life. Doesn't Paul clearly state that salvation is by grace through faith, apart from works (Eph 2:8-9)? Why, then, would theologians label the covenant with Adam the covenant *of works*?

Despite the infelicitous ring of this term to many ears, the covenant of works does not teach that Adam could earn eternal life. Let's start first with the term *covenant*. Adam was not autonomous. He was a created being with whom God made a covenant. This also means that there was absolutely *nothing* that Adam could ever do to merit eternal life, strictly speaking. Apart from the covenant, even if Adam had done all that was required of him, he would still have been an unworthy servant.[7] This is where the concept of a *covenant*, with its attendant promises, is so important. Eternal life was only offered to Adam because God had sovereignly designed to grant eternal life according to the covenantal arrangement. The reward offered was not proportional to Adam's work; nor could Adam put God in his debt. Instead, it was God's sovereign, beneficent, covenantal design to offer Adam much more than he, a creature, could ever earn.

Additionally, for Adam to realize the goal of eternal life offered to him in the covenant, he had to be *perfectly* and *fully* obedient. Another common misconception is that Adam was only bound to *one* act of obedience (not

---

[7]Bavinck, *RD*, 2:570; see also Irenaeus, *Against Heresies*, 4.14.1.

eating from the tree of the knowledge of good and evil). However, that is not the case. Instead, Adam was to be fruitful, multiply, and serve in the Garden (Gen 1:28; 2:15). He was required to love and obey God entirely. He was to serve God as prophet, priest, and king.[8] That is, Adam was entrusted with the revelation of God (prophet), he was to serve in the sanctuary of the Garden of Eden (priest), and was created in God's image as one with dominion over creation (king). The command not to eat from the tree of the knowledge of good and evil (Gen 2:17) was a special, probationary test that summed up all that was required of Adam. To use modern language, Adam was required to obey the moral law of God entirely.[9]

The necessity of Adam's perfect obedience for eternal life is crucial for understanding law and covenant in Scripture. Whatever title one wants to give this first covenant, it establishes early in Scripture the coordination of law keeping and life. The pattern is already evident that blessing follows upon obedience, whereas curse follows upon disobedience. This needs to be appreciated as fully as possible, since so often law keeping (in the theological sense) is considered primarily to be a burden. The law is indeed prominently portrayed as a slave master to drive us to Christ (e.g., Rom 7:10; Gal 3:23). But there is also a fundamental sense in which law keeping leads to blessing. This continues to be true, even though we cannot obey God's law perfectly.

The covenantal condition of Adam's perfect obedience is also foundational for understanding why Jesus had to be perfectly obedient to gain for us eternal life. Perfect obedience continues to be required for eternal life, even after Adam's fall.[10] Yet Adam's sin has consequences for all those born naturally after him. No natural person is able to be perfectly obedient, for all are born sinners. This is evident in Paul's logic in Romans and Galatians, where he outlines the absurdity of trying to meet the requirement of perfection in a postfall world (e.g., Gal 3:10). This is why salvation requires Jesus to obey God perfectly. Additionally, in Jesus himself we see the way that perfect law keeping leads to fullness of life. Jesus was the perfect law

---

[8]Benjamin L. Gladd, *From Adam and Israel to the Church: A Biblical Theology of the People of God*, ESBT (Downers Grove, IL: IVP Academic, 2019), 12-19; Bavinck, *RD*, 3:331.

[9]I will say more about the moral law in chapter two.

[10]Bavinck, *RD*, 3:225.

keeper who delighted fully in the law of God (Ps 1:2) and offers rest for weary souls (Mt 11:28-30).

In summary, if Adam would have fully obeyed God and passed the probationary test, he would have lived forever. We know, however, that he did not pass this test. And the ramifications of his sin did not only affect him, but all who have come after him.

The first head of humanity. Now that we've seen the contours of the covenant with Adam, we should pause to consider some implications in greater detail. It's crucial that we start at the beginning. Too often studies of biblical theology that consider the topics of covenant and law begin later—often with Abraham. Certainly Abraham is important, but we must start where the Bible starts; we must start with Adam.

It's important to affirm Adam was the first human being. I'm aware that this is a hotly debated point today, but despite attempts to downplay the role of Adam or treat this question as inconsequential, the stakes are enormously high. Covenant and law, in particular, are significantly affected by whether one views Adam as a real, historical person, created upright in the image of God with the law of God on his heart and the prospect of eternal life before him. The New Testament has no reservations in speaking of Adam as the first person and speaks frequently of Christ's person and work as the answer to Adam's sin. Put simply, I believe Scripture requires us to affirm that Adam was the first person. This is an especially important point for those who hold to the authority and clarity of Scripture. Genesis 1–2 states that Adam was the first man. Hosea most likely refers to Adam (Hos 6:7). Adam is the first person listed in the genealogy of 1 Chronicles (1 Chron 1:1), and the last person listed in Luke's genealogy (Lk 3:38). Jesus alludes to Adam as the first person (Mt 19:4-5). Paul speaks of Adam on several occasions as a real person (Acts 17:26; Rom 5:12-21; 1 Cor 15:22, 45; 1 Tim 2:13-14). Jude, the half-brother of Jesus, speaks of Adam as a historical person (Jude 14).

This point is not trivial. Since Adam was the first person, it means that the covenant God made with Adam applies to all people (excluding only Jesus).[11]

---

[11]Jesus' virginal conception (i.e., the virgin birth) was an interruption of the normal process of procreation. Jesus is truly human but is not represented by Adam's covenant headship. Instead, the birth of Jesus marks a new creation (see Rom 5:12-21).

This means that all people who have ever lived (apart from Jesus) have Adam as a representative, covenant head whose actions are counted to them. There is no person who is not under obligation to obey God, and no one to whom the requirement of perfect obedience to God's law does not apply.

As the first person and progenitor of all humanity, Adam has a distinctive, unique role in Scripture. The Bible speaks of two heads of humanity in Scripture—two key figures for understanding salvation, and the related themes of covenant and law. Those two figures are Adam and Christ, as we see from the explanation of the apostle Paul (esp. Rom 5:12-21). If we had to boil down the biblical story to two figures, they must be Adam and Christ. Puritan Thomas Goodwin (1600–1680) captured Paul's point well: Paul speaks of Adam and Christ as if there had never been anyone else in the world; for these two men have all other people hanging from their belts.[12] This means that those hanging from their belts include other important figures with whom God makes covenants, like Noah, Abraham, Moses, and David.

It's also important to recognize that Adam was not created already experiencing the highest, most blessed life. He stood with the goal of greater life before him.[13] The fancy term for this is *eschatology*. Eschatology is often associated with the end of the world. This is valid, but eschatology is a rich concept that applies much more extensively to the teaching of Scripture as a whole. Eschatology is quite important for understanding law and covenant, for covenants have in view a final goal. This is also true for the covenant with Adam. If Adam were obedient to the stipulations of the covenant, then he would have inherited *eschatological* eternal life (e.g., Gen 3:22). This becomes even clearer in the New Testament, where eternal life granted by Christ is cast in Adamic terms (e.g., Rom 5:12-21; 1 Cor 15:21-28, 45-49).

Though Adam failed to meet the requirements of the covenant of works, the goal of eternal life remains. After his sin, Adam cannot realize this goal by his own imperfect obedience. So, God graciously intervenes to redeem Adam and his posterity. The eschatological goal of eternal life does not pass

---

[12]This is my paraphrase of Thomas Goodwin, *The Works of Thomas Goodwin*, vol. 4, *Christ Set Forth* (Edinburgh: James Nichol, 1862), 31; see also F. F. Bruce, *Romans*, 2nd ed., TNTC (Grand Rapids, MI: Eerdmans, 1985), 120.

[13]See, e.g., Vos, *Biblical Theology*, 28.

away after Adam's sin, and the subsequent covenants in Scripture move us closer to the goal of final redemption in Jesus Christ.

Adam and the covenant of grace. My kids have asked me on more than one occasion, "Did Adam believe in God?" To put it starkly, if a bit anachronistically, what they are asking is, "Was Adam a Christian?" It's a good question. Adam's actions brought sin into the world. He is culpable for his sin. Further, the New Testament's contrast between Adam and Christ certainly presents Adam as the foil to Christ. And yet the contrast between Adam and Christ deals preeminently with their unique roles as covenant heads, not with Adam's eternal state.

Stated more positively, though Adam failed epically in the beginning, he is also offered redemption from a gracious, covenantal God. Since Adam fails to meet the requirements of the first covenant but is later is portrayed as a faithful covenant member, God must have made a second covenant to save Adam (and Eve, and all who believe). This is what is often known as the *covenant of grace*.[14]

Evidence for the covenant of grace is found in Genesis 3:15, a verse that has often been known as the protevangelium, or proto-gospel, where God promises to save Adam and Eve by means of the seed of the woman: "I will put enmity between you and the woman, / and between your offspring and her offspring; / he shall bruise your head, / and you shall bruise his heel" (Gen 3:15).

Here God speaks to the serpent, who tempted Adam and Eve to sin, about a coming conflict—which will soon begin—between the serpent and the offspring of the woman. The serpent will succeed in damaging this seed to a limited extent (bruising his heel), but the seed of the woman will in the end destroy the serpent (crushing his head). God also provides coverings for Adam and Eve in the Garden, to hide their shame and nakedness (Gen 3:21). It is possible that the skins came from animals that were sacrificed for Adam and Eve.[15] Regardless of how we understand the skins, it's clear that God provides for Adam and Eve.

---

[14]See John D. Currid, "Adam and the Beginning of the Covenant of Grace," in *Covenant Theology: Biblical, Theological, and Historical Perspectives*, ed. Guy Prentiss Waters, J. Nicholas Reid, and John R. Muether (Wheaton, IL: Crossway, 2020), 99-109; see also Irenaeus, *Against Heresies* 3.23.

[15]See Bruce K. Waltke with Cathi J. Fredricks, *Genesis: A Commentary* (Grand Rapids, MI: Zondervan, 2002), 95; contrast Vos, *Biblical Theology*, 156-57.

Evidence for the covenant of grace is also found in the portrayals of Adam as a man of faith after his sin. After sin entered the world, Adam gives his wife the name "Eve," which means she is the mother of all living (Gen 3:20). This is more than a biological statement; this is a statement of faith in God who brings about new life from the death and curse introduced by humanity.[16]

Consistent with this naming, Adam's life after the fall shows that Adam was a redeemed man who lived faithfully in covenant with God, even though he broke the initial covenant. Adam and Eve originally had two sons: Cain and Abel. After Cain murders Abel (Gen 4:8), Adam and Eve are given another son, whom Eve names Seth (from the Hebrew for *put* or *place*; Gen 4:25). God has given them a new son in place of Abel. This naming is also a statement of faith from Eve.

The faith of Adam and Eve is also apparent in the identification of Seth as their offspring, or *seed* (*zeraʾ*). This term is found in the promise of redemption in Genesis 3:15, and in Genesis 4:25 it begins to be fulfilled. From Adam and Eve come two family lines: covenant keepers and covenant breakers. Covenant keepers are the godly seed who will eventually lead to the climactic seed of the woman (Christ himself). Covenant breakers are the seed of the serpent who reject God's authority. Covenant keepers listen to and obey God. Thus, covenant keeping and law keeping go hand in hand. In contrast, the seed of the serpent are those who break covenant and disregard God's authority.

In many ways Genesis (and the rest of Scripture) is a story about the conflict between these two lines.[17] Already the conflict between Cain and Abel demonstrates the divergence of two family lines. God accepted Abel and his sacrifice, but Cain and his sacrifice were rejected (Gen 4:3-7). This was not arbitrary on God's part but reveals the heart of each man (Heb 11:4). Abel was a main of faith who kept covenant; Cain was a man of the devil: a covenant breaker who murdered his brother (1 Jn 3:12; see also Jude 11).

After the account of Cain and Abel comes a genealogy of Cain's family line, which is also a spiritual genealogy. From Cain's line comes an Enoch, who had

---

[16]See also Bavinck, *RD*, 3:200.

[17]The following paragraphs are adapted from Brandon D. Crowe, *The Message of the General Epistles in the History of Redemption: Wisdom from James, Peter, John, and Jude* (Phillipsburg, NJ: P&R, 2015), 108-9; see also Waltke, *Genesis*, 112-13.

a city named after him (Gen 4:17), and a Lamech, who was an adulterer and a murderer (Gen 4:18-24). In contrast to Cain's genealogy is that of Adam's line via Seth. Seth's line also includes an Enoch and a Lamech. However, the Lamech in Seth's line looks to the Lord for deliverance and is the father of Noah (Gen 5:29). Similarly, the Enoch of Seth's line walked closely with God and never dies (Gen 5:22-24; Heb 11:5). These contrasts between two Enochs and two Lamechs illustrate the overarching contrast in the line of Cain and the line of Seth. It is Seth's family line who calls on the name of the Lord (Gen 4:26).[18] This trajectory is also evident in the contrasts between Ishmael and Isaac, and Esau and Jacob, which I will discuss in the next chapter.

In these early chapters of Genesis, obedience is correlated to worship of the true God, and thus to covenant keeping. Genuine covenant members obey the LORD. This is true even *before* the Mosaic law was given. Even before Moses, God's people (and indeed, all people) had some awareness of God's requirements. In the beginning Adam was created righteous (Eccles 7:29), and as such he had the law of God written on his heart. In the New Testament Paul states that all people know to some degree what God requires (see Rom 1:18-32; see also Rom 2:14-15). Cain and the ungodly Lamech knew that they should not murder (Gen 4:7-8, 23-24). Lamech's decision to take two wives was a deviation from God's design in the beginning (Gen 2:24; see also Mt 19:4-6). Later in Genesis Abraham obeyed the commandments, statutes, and law of God (Gen 26:5), even though the law of God had not yet been given through Moses. Scripture is a bit fuzzy on the details of these early laws before the law of Moses, but all people are created in the image of God and are obligated to obedience. Even before the Mosaic law was given, all people, to some degree, knew the law later inscribed in the Ten Commandments. Such laws were, at the least, inscribed on the conscience of all those created in the image of God,[19] though true worshipers of God may well have had a clearer apprehension of God's requirements.

God requires full obedience, but everyone born naturally since Adam is a sinner. The covenant of grace speaks of the way that God provides an answer to sin and a gracious way to covenant fellowship for sinful humanity.

---

[18]Compare Waltke, *Genesis*, 101.
[19]See the extended discussions in Bavinck, *RD*, 3:129-33; Turretin, *Inst.* 11.1 (2:1-7); 11.2.17 (2:12).

Once Adam failed and sin entered the world, then no one who was descended naturally from Adam could meet the covenantal requirement of perfect obedience for eternal life. Even so, the requirement had not been dissolved. From Genesis 3:15 onward, we see God providing a gracious way of salvation for his people—a covenant of grace with Christ as its representative, or head. All subsequent covenants are thus to be understood in relation to this overarching covenant of grace (see figure 1.1).

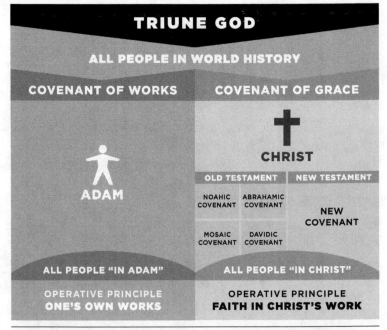

Figure 1.1. Two overarching covenants: covenant of works and covenant of grace[20]

This covenant of grace begins immediately after the fall of Adam.[21] Note, for example, that God tells Adam and Eve that on the day they ate the fruit they would surely die (Gen 2:17). Yet this sanction is delayed, and they do not die immediately. To be sure, there is death for Adam and Eve in a spiritual

---

[20]Though true believers were saved by faith from Adam to Noah as participants in the covenant of grace, I have not listed the Adamic covenant under the covenant of grace since the Adamic covenant usually refers to the covenant of works.

[21]Bavinck, *RD*, 3:197.

sense,[22] but the physical consequences are not immediately enforced. This delay shows the grace of God and the offer of redemption for covenant breakers. Crucially, the covenant of grace involves a Mediator—the seed of the woman (Gen 3:15)—whom we will learn more about as we progress further into the biblical narrative.[23] The New Testament identifies the Mediator as Jesus Christ, the eternal Son of God. When Christ comes in the fullness of time, he does what Adam failed to do: fulfill the requirement for perfect obedience, yielding eternal life. In fact, even though the incarnation of Christ is still future in Genesis, since the covenant of grace applies to all of God's true, believing people in every age, all true believers (including those in the Old Testament) are saved by faith in Christ. Knowledge of Christ is much more shadowy in the Old Testament but is already there in seed form as early as Genesis 3:15.

But before we come to the work of Christ in the New Testament and the way that law and covenant faithfulness dwelt together in perfect harmony, we need to consider the progressively revealed covenants that lead us there.

COVENANT AND LAW WITH NOAH

The context of Noah. The next covenant in Scripture after Adam is the covenant made with Noah. To understand the covenant with Noah, we need to understand that rampant wickedness was the reason for the flood that wiped out every living thing on earth, aside from those in the ark. Genesis 6:5 states, "The LORD saw that the wickedness of man was great in the earth, and that every intention of the thoughts of his heart was only evil continually" (see also Gen 6:11-13). Instead of people offering God the obedience they owed, those who had been created by God had turned their backs on him. The enticingly brief narrative in Genesis 6 that provides the context for this statement has been discussed ad nauseam. It speaks of the sons of God taking the daughters of men as their wives, which happened in the days of the Nephilim. This account is often understood to refer to the sexual sin of angels (= sons of God) who desired (human) women and took them as wives, thus blurring the distinctions and boundaries between angels and humans. Yet despite the popularity of this view, it is not clear from Scripture itself,

---

[22]So, e.g., Waltke, *Genesis*, 87-88.
[23]See Turretin, *Inst.* 12.2.11 (2:176-77); Bavinck, *RD*, 3:215.

and the emphasis in Genesis 6 is clearly on the culpability of *humanity* for sin.[24] Though fallen angels may have somehow played a role in the sin recounted in Genesis 6—perhaps by influencing the actions of wicked kings (i.e., the "sons of God")[25]—the catastrophic flood was a result of *humanity's* persistent sinfulness.

In contrast to this sinful trajectory stands Noah, a righteous man (Gen 6:8-9; see also 2 Pet 2:5). Noah avoids the path of wickedness and walks in the ways of God. Consistent with Noah's righteous way of life is the way he listens to and obeys God, building the ark that would provide safety for him and his family (see 1 Pet 3:20). Noah's obedience brings blessing, whereas the path of wickedness leads to destruction.

Despite Noah's righteousness, it would be a mistake to conclude that he did not need a Redeemer. This is a significant misunderstanding of what truly counts as "righteous" before God—eternal life requires *perfect* righteousness, something that Noah certainly did not qualify for as a descendant of Adam (and as Noah's later drunken sin confirms; see Gen 9:21).[26] Instead, Noah found favor (or, grace) in the eyes of God, which must have come by faith (Gen 6:8; see also Heb 11:7).[27] Noah needed God's saving grace no less than Adam, Abraham, or Peter. God's requirement that perfect obedience is necessary for eternal life still stands; it was not abrogated after the sin of Adam. Adam sinned and could not meet it; neither could Noah. For them to inherit eternal life, someone else had to meet that requirement—their Mediator. To see how this plays out, we must read on.

The covenant with Noah. God also enters into a covenant with Noah.[28] In Genesis 6:18 God states that he will establish his covenant with Noah, who

---

[24]See, e.g., Vos, *Biblical Theology*, 46-49, 52; Simon J. Kistemaker, *Exposition of the Epistles of Peter and the Epistle of Jude*, NTC (Grand Rapids, MI: Baker Book House, 1987), 377-88; Bavinck, *RD*, 2:456-57.

[25]See Waltke, *Genesis*, 115-17; D. A. Carson, "2 Peter" and "Jude," in *Commentary on the New Testament Use of the Old Testament*, ed. G. K. Beale and D. A. Carson (Grand Rapids, MI: Baker Academic, 2007), 1049-51, 1070-72.

[26]See Waltke, *Genesis*, 148-49.

[27]Bruce K. Waltke with Charles Yu, *An Old Testament Theology: An Exegetical, Canonical, and Thematic Approach* (Grand Rapids, MI: Zondervan, 2007), 286.

[28]That God enters into a covenant with Noah is not debated in the way that the covenant with Adam is, though there is some debate about whether God makes one or two covenants with

is then saved (along with his family) in the ark. Later a covenant with Noah is discussed at greater length (Gen 9:1-17). Genesis 9 contains much more detail, including an echo of the command given to Adam and Eve in the beginning to be fruitful and multiply (Gen 9:7; see also Gen 1:28), and the covenant sign of God's (rain)bow (Gen 9:13-17). In Genesis 9 God specifically promises stability in the created order: seasons will persist, and the earth will yield its produce in perpetuity (Gen 8:21-22; 9:8-11). God rules the world and ensures it will be suitable for life as long as the earth endures.[29]

Most of the biblical covenants between God and humanity after Adam are "redemptive" covenants, in which God promises specifically to redeem his people. Yet the covenant with Noah appears to have a more universal emphasis. It relates to all of creation, not just to God's people. This universal emphasis in Genesis 8–9 leads some to refer to the Noahic covenant as a covenant of common grace or a covenant of preservation.[30] This is because the promises to Noah and his offspring benefit all humanity, not only one family line (as we will see with Abraham in what follows).

At the same time, there does seem to be a redemptive element to the Noahic covenant. For not only is humanity in general saved from the flood through Noah, but more specifically God's promised seed is preserved (see Gen 3:15). If the entire world had been wiped out, then the promised seed of the woman could not have come. *But by saving Noah and making a covenant with him and his posterity (Gen 9:9), the godly line of Seth is preserved.* Later Genesis speaks of God's covenant with Abraham and the blessings that come to his family, leading ultimately to Christ himself. This family line comes from Noah and specifically through his son Shem, who was preserved in the ark. This is consistent with how 1 Peter 3:20-21 speaks of Noah's ark as a type, or anticipation, of redemption in Christ.[31] God's promise and provision of a

---

Noah. I will simply refer to one Noahic covenant, inclusive of both Gen 6 and 9, recognizing a diversity of opinion.

[29]See Thomas R. Schreiner, *Covenant and God's Purpose for the World*, SSBT (Wheaton, IL: Crossway, 2017), 35-36.

[30]See Schreiner, *Covenant*, 31; Jonty Rhodes, *Covenants Made Simple: Understanding God's Unfolding Promises to His People* (Phillipsburg, NJ: P&R, 2014), 46-51.

[31]See William J. Dumbrell, *Covenant and Creation: A Theology of Old Testament Covenants* (Grand Rapids, MI: Baker, 1993), 41; see also Meredith G. Kline, *Kingdom Prologue* (Overland Park, KS: Two Age Press, 2000), 240-41.

stable world benefits all people, but God's people stand to gain the most, for to them is given the promise of a Redeemer.[32]

The Noahic covenant marks the end of the world that was and the re-creation of the world—the world that now is (2 Pet 2:5; 3:5-7). When the world is renewed with Noah, the commands given to Noah echo commands given to Adam in the beginning. Many see Noah as a new Adam—here is another man in covenant with God, who is commanded to be fruitful and multiply. Noah also stands at the beginning of a new creation and through him humanity is relaunched. Yet differences between Adam and Noah abound as well. Noah was born a sinner, and the effects of Adam's sin are not undone by Noah. Though in the Noahic covenant God promises to restrain sin for the benefit of the world and his covenant people,[33] the Noahic covenant does not deal with sin definitively. That will come later.

The commands to Noah. Along with God's gracious provision of life, the covenant with Noah also includes specific commands. Noah and his family are to be fruitful and multiply on the earth (Gen 9:1). They are also to exercise dominion, as Adam and Eve were in the beginning (Gen 9:2; see also Gen 1:28). We also find some new commands with Noah. God gives Noah and his descendants every living thing for food, just as he gave them plants earlier (Gen 9:3). It is not entirely clear whether this is the first time God gives people meat to eat or he is simply now reinstituting and regulating this practice.[34] The LORD goes on to say that they may not eat any food with its life (that is, the blood) in it, presumably meaning that people were not to eat living animals, as animals themselves might do.[35]

After this, the LORD turns to the dignity of human life: no one must shed the blood of another person. This is then stated memorably in poetic form.[36] Table 1.1 provides a rather wooden translation, mirroring the structure of the Hebrew.

---

[32]See similarly O. Palmer Robertson, *The Christ of the Covenants* (Phillipsburg, NJ: P&R, 1980), 111, 121-22.
[33]Bavinck, *RD*, 3:218.
[34]The former view is more common; for the latter view see Bavinck, *RD*, 2:575-76, following John Calvin, *Commentaries on the First Book of Moses Called Genesis*, trans. John King, 2 vols. (1923; repr., Grand Rapids, MI: Baker, 2003), 1:291-92.
[35]Vos, *Biblical Theology*, 53.
[36]This structure is commonly recognized.

Table 1.1. Structure of Genesis 9:6

GEN 9:6A (AUTHOR'S TRANS.)	GEN 9:6A (HEBREW)
The one who sheds	šōpēk
the blood	dam
of man	hā'ādām
by man*	bā'ādām
his blood	dāmô
shall be shed	yiššāpēk

*I have opted for the translation "man" (rather than "humanity") for the Hebrew 'ādām given the likely echo of Adam and the original created order in this passage.

No one is to take the life of another person. The reason for this is stated in the second half of the verse: all people are made in the image of God (Gen 9:6). This is traced back to Adam, the first man who was made upright in God's image (Gen 1:26-27). Just as Adam was made in the image of God, so too all humanity descending from him is made in God's image—even after the entrance of sin into the world. To take the life of another human is not only injustice of the gravest kind against another person, but it is also an attack on the God in whose image that person has been made.[37] This also presents a clear contrast to the way humans relate to the animal world: animals can be killed for food, but no one is allowed to take the life of another person. Instead of taking life, Noah and his offspring are commanded to be fruitful and increase on the earth (Gen 9:7).

Though it can be easy to overlook the commands given to Noah, they are foundational for the sustenance of life in the re-created, postflood world. Humanity is confirmed in its dignity and authority over the created realm and is commanded again to fill the earth. The institution of capital punishment for murder also underscores the dignity of humanity. God sets up the postfall world to promote and sustain life, and it is incumbent upon all people to live in a way consistent with that. Life is to be promoted in the new world order; murder is expressly forbidden. Indeed, so valuable is human life that

---

[37]See also Vos, *Biblical Theology*, 54.

to guard its sanctity, an offender's life is required if someone takes the life of another person. This does not, however, give license to individuals to take matters into their own hands. Instead, this is the role of governments (Rom 13:4). For as Jesus makes clear, it is not right for individuals to demand vengeance for personal wrongs (Mt 5:38-42; see also Rom 12:19-21).

The laws given to Noah, just like the covenant itself, apply to all of creation and abide in perpetuity.[38] Thus, we are always to be fruitful and fill the earth. Murder is always prohibited, and the death penalty is to be enforced where this command is transgressed. We are also to respect the lives of animals. These commands are given at the re-creation of the world and are not part of the theocratic law of Israel that entails civil and ceremonial dimensions (more on those in subsequent chapters). This means that the commands to Noah remain in effect even after the coming of Christ. Humanity already knew that murder was wrong. This is not a new development, but it is a confirmation, progression, and further explanation of what was already known. And this also comes in the context of a sovereignly established covenant, designed for the flourishing of humanity and the entire created realm. And, as in all biblical covenants, the ultimate goal is for the praise, honor, and glory of God: "For from him and through him and to him are all things. To him be glory forever. Amen" (Rom 11:36).

CONCLUSION AND APPLICATION

The beginning of Scripture is crucial for understanding what follows. Despite the brevity of the accounts with Adam and Noah, they are some of the most important chapters for understanding the Bible. The covenants and laws given to Adam and Noah are assumed by later biblical writers. The New Testament's discussions of the work of Christ and its implications for life assume the covenantal and creational contours of Genesis 1–9 (see figure 1.2).

Studying covenant and law reminds us that the Bible is a practical book; the Bible shows us how God relates to us and how we are to live in covenant with him. It is therefore fitting that we consider points of application in each

---

[38]See similarly John Murray, *Principles of Conduct: Aspects of Biblical Ethics* (Grand Rapids, MI: Eerdmans, 1957), 109-22.

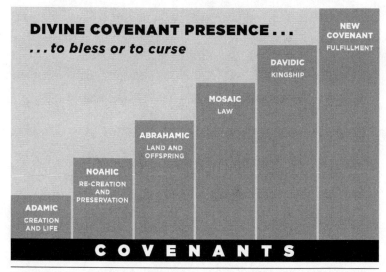

Figure 1.2. Biblical-theological approach to covenants

chapter of this study. Five key takeaways from these opening chapters of Genesis include the following:

1. God is the Creator; we are creatures. We are dependent on God for everything, and we owe him our lives and our obedience. Obedience is not "extra"; it is what God requires of all people. The God of Scripture is also the one true God of the whole world. He created everyone, and everyone's roots are traced back to Adam, which explains the unity of the human race.

2. God is a gracious and covenantal God. He desires to have fellowship with humanity and even offers us a reward. In this, God takes the initiative and promises more than we can ever deserve. When Adam failed, God immediately intervened to implement the covenant of grace to save Adam and his descendants who believe. He likewise rescued Noah and his family for their benefit but also for the benefit of all humanity. Further, in the covenant of grace God ensures that the conditions of the covenant are met.[39]

---

[39]Bavinck, *RD*, 3:266; see also Waltke, *Old Testament Theology*, 255.

3. God rules over the world. This is God's providence: he governs all his creatures and all their actions. God is not the author of sin, yet sin does not take him by surprise. When Adam introduced sin and when sin increased rampantly on the earth, God intervened to save his people and renew the world. The doctrine of providence is especially comforting for God's people since he governs the world with a particular eye to his people. In the words of John Calvin, "the principle purpose of Biblical history is to teach that the Lord watches over the ways of the saints with such great diligence that they do not even stumble over a stone."[40]

4. God works through families. We see this in the contrast between the ungodly lineage of Cain and the godly lineage of Seth. Disobedience often begets disobedience; obedience often begets obedience. We also see this in the way that Noah *and his family* were saved from the flood by means of the ark. This pattern will continue throughout Scripture, and even provides parents motivation and comfort in the rearing of children: the covenant promises keep the next generation in view. Even so, physical lineage does not guarantee covenant fidelity, for from the same family come covenant breakers and covenant keepers. We should pray with and for our children, teaching them the ways of God that they may turn to him and choose the path of life.

5. God is the author of all life, and human life is especially sacred. We must live in a way that reflects this sanctity of life. Are we doing all we can to promote and protect life? Are we standing up for the vulnerable and the weakest among us? Jesus explains in the parable of the Good Samaritan that it's not sufficient to ask, "Who is my neighbor?" in order to lessen our responsibility for others. Instead, our task is to *be a neighbor* to those around us—even those that may seem to be out of the scope of neighborliness (Lk 10:36-37).[41]

This mindset has all sorts of ramifications, not least with respect to those who appear to be different from us. Every person, everywhere,

---

[40]John Calvin, *Institutes of the Christian Religion*, ed. John T. McNeill, trans. Ford Lewis Battles, 2 vols., LCC 20-21 (Louisville, KY: Westminster John Knox, 1960), 1.17.6 (1:218).

[41]See Richard B. Hays, *The Moral Vision of the New Testament—Community, Cross, New Creation: A Contemporary Introduction to New Testament Ethics* (San Francisco: Harper, 1996), 451.

is made in the image of God. We must love our neighbor, and there is no one who is not our neighbor. This applies to everyone, such as those we might consider different from ourselves, those who are not important or "useful" in the eyes of the world, those from other countries or ethnicities, those who are weak or marginalized, those who are incarcerated, those who are in the womb—as well as those who are rich and powerful. We must respect the value and dignity of *every* human life.[42] The laws given to Noah do not provide answers for every scenario, but they provide a framework. All life is sacred, and our actions must reflect this priority.

SUGGESTED READING

Schreiner, Thomas R. *Covenant and God's Purpose for the World.* SSBT. Wheaton, IL: Crossway, 2017.

Vos, Geerhardus. *Biblical Theology: Old and New Testaments.* 1948. Reprint, Edinburgh: Banner of Truth, 1975.

Waltke, Bruce K. with Charles Yu. *An Old Testament Theology: An Exegetical, Canonical, and Thematic Approach.* Grand Rapids, MI: Zondervan, 2007.

---

[42]For further discussion, see Murray, *Principles of Conduct,* 178-79. Genesis 9 does not prohibit self-defense or just war, both of which are legitimate.

Chapter Two

THE FAMILY

ABRAHAM AND HIS CHILDREN

ONE OF THE STRIKING THINGS about the biographies of famous people is how ordinary their beginnings often were. Walt Disney struggled with consistent work as an aspiring artist, often going without food, and headed to Hollywood with hardly anything to his name. Michael Jordan was not always a basketball legend, and once he did not make his high school basketball team. As an unknown author J. K. Rowling worked on the first Harry Potter book in local Edinburgh coffee shops. Yet all these became masters at their crafts, establishing benchmarks for excellence and making a worldwide impact. Even so, they were once beginners like everyone else.

It can be easy to forget the humble beginnings of people who seem to be larger than life. This is also true for the next major character we meet in Scripture after Noah: Abram (later Abraham). There was nothing particularly special about Abram, but God called him to be the father of a new nation. From this call eventually blossoms a large covenant family from which comes Christ, and through whom comes the blessing to all the families of the earth. Abraham did not earn his salvation by law keeping but was declared righteous by faith alone (Gen 15:6), which is a crucial tenet in understanding the relationship of law and covenant in Scripture. Though Abraham was justified by faith, he also manifests the obedience that becomes true children of God.

THE CALL

After God's covenant with Noah, Genesis speaks of the repopulation of the earth and provides a genealogy of the peoples, known as the Table of Nations (Gen 10:1-32). These descend from the three sons of Noah: Shem, Ham, and Japheth. From the line of Shem comes a man of Ur named Terah, along with his son, Abram (Gen 11:10-32). They leave the land of Ur of the Chaldeans (in modern-day Iraq) and set out on their way to Canaan. But they end up staying in Haran (in modern-day Turkey). Terah's family is not particularly noteworthy; nothing indicates they worshiped the true God (see Josh 24:2). Yet this family will become the most important family in covenant history.

God takes the initiative by calling Abram away from his family to a place that God would show him. Genesis 12:1-3 records this important text for understanding covenant and law:

> Now the LORD said to Abram, "Go from your country and your kindred and your father's house to the land that I will show you. And I will make of you a great nation, and I will bless you and make your name great, so that you will be a blessing. I will bless those who bless you, and him who dishonors you I will curse, and in you all the families of the earth shall be blessed."

God promises to make Abram's family a great nation that will bless all the families of the earth, which is perhaps surprising since Abram and Sarai had no children of their own. Sarai's barrenness, included in the genealogy of Terah (Gen 11:30), stands in sharp relief to the pattern of childbearing in the other genealogies thus far in Genesis. God promises to bless Abram, his family, and those who honor Abram. On the other hand, those who dishonor Abram will be cursed. The language of blessing and curse becomes standard language for the benefits and repercussions of covenants: those who keep covenant are blessed; those who turn their back on the covenant are cursed.

The reason Abram's family is the most important family in covenant history pertains to the promise of offspring to Abram. This is implied in Genesis 12:1-3 but is stated more explicitly in Genesis 12:7: God would provide offspring for Abram—even though he was already seventy-five years old (Gen 12:4). Next, God promises Abram a land (Gen 15:7-21) and confirms this with a covenant ceremony. This ceremony sounds quite foreign to modern ears. Abram brings a three-year-old cow, a three-year-old ram, a turtledove, and a pigeon before the LORD. The animals (not the birds) are cut in half and laid on the ground, with Abram protecting them from predators. That night Abram falls into a deep sleep and is overwhelmed with darkness. The LORD promises Abram that his offspring would be slaves for four hundred years, would come out of the land of slavery with much booty, and would possess the land that Abram currently occupied (Gen 15:18-21). To confirm this, God himself passes through the midst of the dead animals in the form of a smoking fire pot and a flaming torch (Gen 15:17). These anticipate God's presence later with his people in the exodus, where he leads them by fire and a pillar of cloud (Ex 13:21-22). This also most likely indicates that God is taking the covenant curses on himself: he is swearing to do what he promised, lest he become like the slaughtered animals.[1]

This covenant ceremony in Genesis 15 highlights two key elements of the Abrahamic covenant that will be important for understanding the rest of the biblical storyline: God promises Abram descendants and land—heirs and an inheritance. These are not given to Abram on account of any inherent righteousness in him, but in accord with his faith in God's Word. These two elements—seed and land—will be staples of God's covenants with his people. At the same time, these are not entirely new. They are already anticipated in Genesis 12 and echo God's earlier covenants with Adam and Noah. Yet with Abram comes much more specificity with the working out of the promise of the seed of the woman who will crush the serpent (Gen 3:15). For now we see that this seed will come specifically through Abram's family line.

---

[1]So, e.g., Bruce K. Waltke with Cathi J. Fredricks, *Genesis: A Commentary* (Grand Rapids, MI: Zondervan, 2001), 244-45; Gordon J. Wenham, *Genesis 1–15*, WBC 1 (Nashville: Thomas Nelson, 1987), 332.

The covenant. In Genesis 15 comes the first explicit mention of a covenant with Abram. The LORD appears to Abram, telling him not to fear and promising him a great reward. When Abram responds that he still did not have a child, the LORD confirms that Abram's very own child would indeed be his heir and that his offspring would be as numerous as the stars in the sky (Gen 15:4-5).

At this point comes one of the most consequential statements in all of Scripture about faith: Abram believes the LORD and it is counted to him as righteousness (Gen 15:6). No sinner is declared righteous before God on the basis of his or her own obedience, but righteousness comes by faith. Abram is justified before God by believing God's word, not because of anything he himself does. Even so, the requirement of perfect obedience given to Adam had not been abrogated. Although Abram is counted righteous by faith and inherits the promise of eternal life by faith, his experience of eternal blessedness still requires someone's perfect obedience. Abram's faith thus looked outside of himself to the God who provides the righteousness needed for salvation. The New Testament makes it clear that even Abram was saved by the perfect obedience of Jesus Christ, for there is no other name given by which anyone can be saved.[2]

These same emphases are apparent in Genesis 17, where the LORD gives Abram the covenant sign of circumcision and changes his name from Abram ("exalted father") to Abraham ("father of a multitude"). Again the LORD confirms that Abraham would have many descendants, and even that nations and kings would come from his family line (Gen 17:4-8). The LORD also confirms that the child would come through Sarai (= Sarah), his wife, and not from someone else. It will be specifically through Isaac that all the nations will be blessed (Gen 17:21).[3]

WHAT ABOUT THE LAW?

When the LORD enters into a covenant with Abraham, he also calls him to walk faithfully before him. Several passages are particularly pertinent:[4]

---

[2]E.g., Acts 4:12; 10:43; see also Jn 8:56. The covenant promises in the Old Testament dealt not *primarily* with earthly blessings but with the blessings of eternal life. See further Calvin, *Inst.* 2.10.2-3; Turretin, *Inst.* 12.7.19, 45 (2:222-23, 231-32).

[3]In Genesis 16 Abram conceived a child (Ishmael) with Sarai's servant Hagar, but Ishmael was not the chosen seed.

[4]I have added emphasis in the quotations that follow.

When Abram was ninety-nine years old the LORD appeared to Abram and said to him, "I am God Almighty; *walk before me, and be blameless, that I may make my covenant between me and you, and may multiply you greatly.*" (Gen 17:1-2)

The LORD said, "Shall I hide from Abraham what I am about to do, seeing that Abraham shall surely become a great and mighty nation, and all the nations of the earth shall be blessed in him? For I have chosen him, *that he may command his children and his household after him to keep the way of the LORD by doing righteousness and justice,* so that the LORD may bring to Abraham what he has promised him." (Gen 18:17-19)

[The angel of the LORD] said, "Do not lay your hand on the boy or do anything to him, *for now I know that you fear God, seeing you have not withheld your son, your only son, from me.*" . . . And the angel of the LORD called to Abraham a second time from heaven and said, "By myself I have sworn, declares the LORD, *because you have done this and have not withheld your son, your only son,* I will surely bless you, and I will surely multiply your offspring as the stars of heaven and as the sand that is on the seashore. And your offspring shall possess the gate of his enemies, and in your offspring shall all the nations of the earth be blessed, *because you have obeyed my voice.*" (Gen 22:12, 15-18)

[Spoken to Isaac]: "Sojourn in this land, and I will be with you and will bless you, for to you and to your offspring I will give all these lands, and I will establish the oath that I swore to Abraham your father. I will multiply your offspring as the stars of heaven and will give to your offspring all these lands. And in your offspring all the nations of the earth shall be blessed, *because Abraham obeyed my voice and kept my charge, my commandments, my statutes, and my laws.*" (Gen 26:3-5)

Clearly Abraham is described as a righteous man who obeyed the voice of his covenant God. Yet Abraham's obedience was not the *foundation* of his acceptance before God since Genesis 15:6 states that Abraham's faith in God resulted in righteousness. Abraham's obedience did not earn him a righteous standing before God, though we will see in what follows that

Abraham's faith was indeed a faith that obeyed. Hebrews 11:8 captures it well: "by faith Abraham obeyed."

Yet if Abraham obeyed God, what specific commands did he obey? The apostle Paul makes a big deal about Abraham living 430 years before the law was given (Gal 3:17-18). How then could Abraham live according to the law of God before it was given? What was expected of him?

This is an important question. Even if Scripture does not explain it at length, we have enough information to draw a few conclusions. Even before the law was given through Moses, God had sufficiently made known himself and the righteousness he requires of humanity (see Rom 1:18-32; 2:14-15). Being made in the image of God entails knowledge of who God is and what he requires.

In addition, Abraham received special revelation from God. For example, he was specifically commanded to go to the land God would show him (Gen 12:1), to set up a covenant ceremony, to implement the sign of circumcision (Gen 17:9-14), and to sacrifice his son (Gen 22:1-2). Additionally, the LORD determined to reveal to Abraham what he was about to do to Sodom (Gen 18:17-19). Sodom's unrighteousness was inexcusable—not even ten righteous people were found there—and is contrasted with Abraham's righteousness (Gen 18:19). For Abraham to walk by faith meant walking in the commandments of God.

Abraham is explicitly described in Genesis 26:5 as one who obeyed the LORD's charge, commandments, statutes, and laws. These comprehensive terms could refer to the law of God revealed to the patriarchs—which is not discussed in detail—or they could also refer to the law that would later be codified specifically through Moses.[5] Either way, Abraham lived in accord with the law of God, even though the law given through Moses came 430 years later (more on this in the next chapter).

This realization also helps us navigate a particularly tricky issue that we encounter in Genesis (and elsewhere in the Old Testament): What do we make of the proliferation of wives taken by the patriarchs? Was this lawful for them, or was it wrong? To assess this question, we need to follow the lead of Jesus

---

[5]See Waltke, *Genesis*, 368. Abraham also already knew the law of the tithe; see Gen 14:18-20.

and start at the beginning (Mt 19:4-6). The created order of one man and one woman united in marriage provides the framework for what marriage should be (Gen 2:24). This is the standard, though unfortunately we find many deviations from this pattern dating back to the ungodly Lamech (Gen 4:23). The importance of marriage and the wickedness of adultery was well known already in the days of Genesis. The Pharaoh of Egypt knew it was wrong to take another man's wife (Gen 12:18-19; see Gen 12:12-13), as did Abimelech king of Gerar (Gen 20:2-6).

This means it was wrong for Abraham to father a child by Hagar (Gen 16). Though it was undoubtedly difficult, Abraham should have continued to wait by faith, for the LORD would fulfill his promise to Abraham by means of his wife. Abraham's liaison with Hagar led to heartache and conflict on various levels. Paul will later use this example to illustrate the wrongheadedness of trying to please God in our own strength, in contrast to living by faith (Gal 4:21-31).

This also means that it was not according to God's design for the patriarchs like Jacob, or kings like David or Solomon, to take multiple wives. Polygamy is a deviation from God's design of one man and one woman. Conflict and idolatry consistently ensue where polygamy is practiced. We should not hesitate to call this sin.[6] This is clearer in the New Testament (see Eph 5:31-32) but is already made known in the Old Testament. Polygamy is included in the prohibition against adultery in the Ten Commandments, which was already known as part of God's moral law.[7]

At the same time, God is gracious. He works even through sinful people. This is clear, for example, in the patriarch Judah's unrighteous desire to sleep with a prostitute (Gen 38). In this case the woman turned out not to be a prostitute but his widowed daughter-in-law Tamar. Though she tricked Judah,

---

[6]See Robert R. Gonzales Jr., "Faults of Our Fathers: The Spread of Sin in the Patriarchal Narratives and its Implications," *WTJ* 74 (2012): 367-86. Levirate marriage, in which a man took his brother's widow to raise up offspring, is commanded (Deut 25:5-10), but this is different from polygamy. Levirate marriage is explicitly for the purpose of raising up offspring for a deceased brother whose name would otherwise be cut off from the covenant community.

[7]God's law also includes manifold ways of caring for those who were vulnerable, such as an unloved wife (Ex 21:7-11) or a woman who had been cast off by her husband (Deut 24:1-4). God also protected and provided for Hagar and Ishmael after they were cast out (Gen 21:12-21).

Tamar was more righteous than Judah, for she was more concerned with furthering the Abrahamic seed than Judah himself (Gen 38:26). And it is through this line of Judah via Tamar that the promised seed will eventually come (see Mt 1:3).

In spite of all the missteps of his people, God remains faithful to his covenant promise to Abraham to make him a great nation and to give him offspring. God would fulfill his promises in his time and in his way, showing that it was his power that was at work. It would be when Sarah was beyond the age of childbearing and Abraham was as good as dead that they were given the promised son (Heb 11:11-12). The LORD provides the offspring for his covenant people, and Abraham's family soon begins to grow and multiply greatly.

THE COVENANT FAMILY GROWS

To appreciate the importance of the growth of Abraham's family, we again need to remember the promise given to Adam and Eve that the offspring of the woman would crush the head of the serpent (Gen 3:15). The term used for offspring is *seed* (Hebrew: *zera'*), which can be either singular or plural. The term is used both ways in Genesis, for Abraham is promised many offspring (Gen 13:15-16; 15:5; 17:7-8), yet this promise will be focused in one offspring in particular (Gen 3:15). This is anticipated with the birth of Isaac (Gen 17:9; 21:12) and will come to fruition through the one man Jesus Christ—the promised seed of the woman who crushes the serpent's head (Gal 3:16; see also Rom 16:20).

The growth of Abraham's family recalls the command originally given to Adam and Eve to be fruitful and multiply; this is becoming a reality through God's covenant with Abraham.[8] The growth of Abraham's family is also related the covenant sign of circumcision. This defining mark of the Abrahamic covenant applied to all males in Abraham's household and to all the male children who would come from his line (Gen 17:10-14). Circumcision was a bloody institution that illustrated the need for cleansing.[9] Since it was applied

---

[8]See Stephen G. Dempster, *Dominion and Dynasty: A Theology of the Hebrew Bible*, NSBT 15 (Downers Grove, IL: InterVarsity Press, 2003), 80-85.

[9]Geerhardus Vos, *Biblical Theology: Old and New Testaments* (1948; repr., Edinburgh: Banner of Truth, 1975), 90.

to the reproductive organ that transmits the physical seed,[10] it may have also reminded the Hebrew people of the promised seed that would come from Abraham's family line. There was nothing magical about circumcision—it was also known in other ancient cultures—but it was a covenant sign that set Abraham's family apart. Yet circumcision was not designed to be merely external. Circumcision represented the righteousness and new life that God bestows by faith to those who trust in him (see also Rom 4:11; Col 2:11-12).[11] Already in the days of Moses physical circumcision represented the spiritual need to be cleansed and renewed (Deut 10:16; 30:6).

Circumcision did not guarantee anyone true faith—it was applied to all males in the covenant community. Even in Abraham's family we find two divergent spiritual legacies, as we saw with the lines of Cain and Seth.[12] Isaac was the child of promise; Ishmael was the child of the flesh. This pattern continues with Jacob and Esau. Both children were born of the same woman (Rebekah), but they were two different nations, and the older would serve the younger according to God's will (Gen 25:21-26). Jacob became Israel and remained covenantally faithful, whereas Esau turned his back on the faith of his fathers, becoming himself the head of Edom who opposed Israel (Num 20:18-21). Covenant fidelity was manifested both in God's choice and in fidelity to the stipulations of the covenant. For example, Esau the firstborn was not favored over Jacob (Gen 25:23; 27:26-40; see also Mal 1:2-3; Rom 9:13). But Esau himself renounced his covenant privileges (Gen 25:29-34; see also Heb 12:16-17) and married wives from other nations (Gen 26:34-35), thus showing his lack of concern for the covenantal offspring of his grandfather Abraham.[13] The family lines of Jacob and Esau represent the seed of the woman and the seed of the serpent.

Abraham is not the beginning of the biblical story, but he opens a new chapter focusing especially on the promises of land and seed. Though God chooses Abraham apart from any goodness in him, Genesis also says that

---

[10]Vos, *Biblical Theology*, 90; Waltke, *Genesis*, 261, 264.

[11]Bavinck, *RD*, 4:499-500.

[12]This paragraph is adapted from Brandon D. Crowe, *The Message of the General Epistles in the History of Redemption: Wisdom from James, Peter, John, and Jude* (Phillipsburg, NJ: P&R, 2015), 109-10.

[13]See also Waltke, *Genesis*, 364-65, 375-76.

God blesses Abraham *because* he kept the commandments of God (Gen 26:5). In the context of the covenant, obedience and blessing go hand in hand. Abraham is a model of faith, showing that faith bears the fruit of obedience. Though Abraham is imperfect, he anticipates Christ, "who by his obedience fulfills the righteous requirements of the law and secures its blessings for his seed."[14] Soon Abraham's family becomes so large that an entire nation has emerged—a nation in need of redemption.

CONCLUSION AND APPLICATION

The role of Abraham in Scripture is crucial for understanding the proper relationship between law and covenant. Paul uses Abraham as the model of faith that believes and is saved even before the law of Moses is given (Gal 3:17-18; see also Rom 4:9-12). Several points of application stand out.

1. Abraham illustrates the way to please God: by faith. By faith Abraham was accepted before God (Gen 15:6). Abraham was seventy-five years old when he left Ur, and Isaac was born twenty-five years later. This is a long time for an aging man—one who was as good as dead (Heb 11:12)—to wait for God's timing. Yet Abraham—imperfect though he was—persisted in his faith in God's promise of an offspring that would bless all the peoples of the earth. And when he was tested in the offering of Isaac, Abraham proved his faith in God—the one whom he believed could even raise the dead (Heb 11:17-19; see also Rom 4:16-22). Walking by faith may mean we do not see the fulfillment of what has been promised in this life; Abraham didn't (Heb 11:13). But faith believes in God's word when it seems unlikely, or even impossible.

   Abraham continues to be the model of faith for New Testament believers as well. Abraham was justified by faith (Rom 4:1-3; see also Gal 3:15-18), and he walked in the ways of God. Abraham shows us the way of the covenant is the way of faith, and this faith manifests itself in obedience to God (Jas 2:20-24).

2. Not everyone who has received the sign of the covenant truly believes and obeys God from the heart. Abraham's line includes both Ishmael

---

[14]Waltke, *Genesis*, 372.

and Isaac, Esau and Jacob. These men were all circumcised, yet circumcision on its own does not profit anyone. What matters is obedience to the God of the covenant (Gal 5:6). Circumcision pointed already in the Old Testament to the circumcision of the heart (Deut 10:16; 30:6), referring to the need for true belief in God's covenant, not merely external membership.

Circumcision is no longer the sign of the covenant; that distinction now belongs to baptism.[15] But the Old Testament warns us that merely receiving the outward sign is not sufficient. All those who are baptized are called to believe in the God of the covenant and commit themselves to walk in his ways. Baptism, like circumcision, is a testimony to God's faithfulness that God bestows righteousness to those who believe (Rom 4:11). Neither baptism nor church attendance guarantees true faith. It is therefore crucial that we "improve" our baptism by reflecting on its true purpose, looking always to Christ by faith.

3. The promise to Abraham of a land of inheritance is much bigger than only a strip of land. Instead, the promise to Abraham was that he would inherit *the entire world* (Rom 4:13). Similarly, Jesus promises his disciples that the meek will inherit *the earth* (Mt 5:6; see also Ps 37:11). Indeed, already in the Old Testament, in both Genesis 15:16 and its echo in Deuteronomy 1:7-8, the scope of the land promised to Abraham was broader than the kingdom of Israel ever realized, even during the Davidic kingdom.[16] This larger vision is anticipated by the Promised Land but is bigger than just the Promised Land. The land of Canaan was only the beginning of the worldwide inheritance promised to God's covenant people by faith. We therefore look ahead to the New Heavens and the New Earth where righteousness dwells (2 Pet 3:13). Those who, like Abraham, walk by faith in the seed of Abraham are granted an everlasting, worldwide inheritance. The land in the Old

---

[15]The New Testament clarifies that circumcision is no longer required for God's people, but baptism is. See, e.g., Acts 2:38-39; Acts 15:1 with 15:19-21, 28-29; Col 2:11-12.

[16]Peter C. Craigie, *The Book of Deuteronomy*, NICOT (Grand Rapids, MI: Eerdmans, 1976), 95-96; Wenham, *Genesis 1–15*, 333; Waltke, *Genesis*, 245; see also Bruce K. Waltke with Charles Yu, *An Old Testament Theology: An Exegetical, Canonical, and Thematic Approach* (Grand Rapids, MI: Zondervan, 2007), 512-87.

Testament looks ahead to the fulfillment of the Abrahamic promise, which is bigger than we may suspect. This will be explained in more detail in the New Testament.

SUGGESTED READING

Alexander, T. D. *From Paradise to the Promised Land: An Introduction to the Pentateuch.* 2nd ed. Grand Rapids, MI: Baker Academic, 2002.

Belcher, Richard P., Jr. *The Fulfillment of the Promises of God: An Explanation of Covenant Theology.* Fearn, Ross-shire: Mentor, 2020.

Redd, John Scott. "The Abrahamic Covenant." In *Covenant Theology: Biblical, Theological, and Historical Perspectives,* edited by Guy Prentiss Waters, J. Nicholas Reid, and John R. Muether, 133-47. Wheaton, IL: Crossway, 2020.

Chapter Three

THE EXODUS

MOSES AND ISRAEL

HOW COULD THOSE WHO HAD GATHERED at Gettysburg know they were witnessing one of the most significant moments in the young nation's history? After the lengthy, two-hour address from the previous speaker, the president of the United States ascended the platform to deliver his own remarks. They lasted only a few minutes and contained fewer than three hundred words. As quickly as he started, he finished. And yet those ten sentences of the Gettysburg Address are remembered not only as the most famous speech of America's best-known president, but they also cast a vision for a struggling nation that recalled its foundational identity.

Abraham Lincoln delivered the Gettysburg Address during the American Civil War, amid a fog of uncertainty. Though now historians look back on the Battle of Gettysburg, which had been fought a few months earlier, as a key turning point of the war, that was not certain when Lincoln addressed the crowd. He did not know when or how the war would end. Yet he knew the young nation was at a crossroads. Caught in the crucible of war, Lincoln reminded his audience of the principles on which America was founded. For the nation to endure and prosper, there had to be a new birth of freedom.

In this chapter we look to the rise of the nation of Israel and the crucible that defined it. From the humble beginnings of one family, Israel grows to become numerous and prosperous in a foreign land. Yet the people of Israel become enslaved with an ever-increasing burden, and they cry out to the LORD for redemption. The LORD hears their cries and delivers them with a mighty arm in the exodus. At this point the people of Israel really become a nation. Israel is defined by its covenant relationship to the LORD who redeemed his people from slavery and gave them his laws that they may serve him and worship him rightly.

The laws that Moses mediates to the people of Israel at Mount Sinai (including but not limited to the Ten Commandments) must be viewed in the context of what has come before. The covenantal, Creator God reveals himself to Abraham and then to Moses. He begins to speak more specifically about one family who becomes one nation, and he shows this family and nation how they are to live in covenant with him. The Mosaic covenant, in particular, highlights God's grace and provision, directing God's people how they should live before him. In fact, the law given through Moses provides Scripture's most thorough exposition of what God requires of us.

At the same time, the law given through Moses is not the final word about the law; the law points ahead to Christ, who fulfills the law and teaches us what the law truly requires. This means that to understand the covenants and law given to Abraham and Moses, we must always remember they inherently point forward to the coming of Christ—the seed of the woman.

THE EMERGENCE OF ISRAEL

Abraham's family line continued to grow, especially through his grandson Jacob (renamed Israel), the father of the Twelve Patriarchs. By the end of Genesis this family had moved to Egypt, where Jacob's son Joseph had risen to become second in charge to Pharaoh himself. In Egypt God protected and provided for his people in the midst of famine, and they continued to become a great people. This is recounted at the beginning of the book of Exodus: "the people of Israel were fruitful and increased greatly; they multiplied and grew exceedingly strong, so that the land was filled with them" (Ex 1:7). The LORD was fulfilling his covenant promises to Abraham.

Yet there was also a problem: the people of Israel had become so numerous and prosperous that they were seen as a threat to Egypt, and there arose a Pharaoh who did not how Joseph saved them in a previous generation. This Pharaoh commanded the murder of all the Israelite newborn sons. If successful, this would wipe out the promised offspring of Abraham and nullify the coming of the promised seed. But it was not successful. Many faithful Israelites—like the midwives Shiphrah and Puah, and Moses' parents—refused to obey Pharaoh's unlawful order at great risk to themselves but in faithfulness to the Abrahamic covenant.

Nevertheless, Israel faced enslavement and ever-increasing burdens. The people needed deliverance and cried out to their God for help. He heard; he redeemed; and he made them a new nation.

Redemption in the exodus. God redeems his people through the exodus. This work of redemption in many ways defines the people of God, and it anticipates the redemption that Christ accomplishes in the New Testament. The exodus is a demonstration of the power of God against apparently overwhelming odds; the God of Moses defeats the Egyptian king, the army of Egypt, and even the so-called gods of Egypt. This is evident not only in the ten plagues against Egypt but preeminently through the deliverance of the multitude of Israel through the Red Sea.

The story of the exodus is familiar. It is also an extremely important part of the Bible for understanding the relationship between law and covenant. For the God who delivers the Israelites is the covenantal God of Abraham, who is also the true God of the whole world. The same God we have met before reveals more about himself in the exodus. In Exodus 3 Moses, who has fled from Egypt after killing an Egyptian, encounters a burning bush at Mount Sinai (a.k.a. Horeb). There the LORD reveals his name to Moses, often translated as "I AM WHO I AM" (Ex 3:14).[1] Though here the LORD explains his name in this way for the first time, the great I AM identifies himself as the covenantal God of previous generations. He is the God of Abraham, Isaac,

---

[1] The name "I AM" is typically translated in English as LORD, using all capital letters.

and Jacob (Ex 3:6, 15-16). In accord with the covenantal promises to Abraham, the LORD promises to deliver his people from bondage and give them the land he promised to Abraham (Ex 3:8, 17).

This covenantal LORD takes the initiative to save his people. Before the Mosaic law is given, the people are redeemed that they may worship the LORD (Ex 4:22-23). This observation is crucial, since too often it is assumed—even by Christians—that the Old Testament is a religion of works whereby the Israelites had to obey the law before God would save them. Not so! In the exodus we see the pattern of redemption, which we also find in the New Testament, that God intervenes to save his people in accord with his faithfulness to his covenant promises. God's people in the Old Testament were saved by faith in Christ, just as believers are today. Likewise, God's people in the Old Testament were called to obey him from the heart, just as we are today.

Of course, there were also differences. The Old Testament speaks with much less clarity about the coming of the Messiah, and Israel's experience of the Holy Spirit and freedom of conscience (i.e., experience of liberation from the bondage and condemnation of sin) were not as profuse. But Israel was not granted salvation on the basis of obedience. There is only one way of salvation. The covenant with Moses—including the law of Moses—must be understood as part of God's one covenant of grace. Moses therefore does not teach a different way of salvation than the New Testament. If only *perfect* obedience meets the standard for eternal life, then no natural person since Adam can meet this requirement. The obedience required of Israel in the law of Moses must therefore be an obedience of faith, not an obedience that would earn salvation (see Rom 9:30-32). God calls Israel, his son, out of Egypt (Ex 4:22-23). And as son of God Israel is required to reflect the character of its divine Father, as we see in greater detail in Deuteronomy.

The pattern of redemption in the exodus—first deliverance ("indicative," what God does for us), then the giving of the law leading to worship ("imperative," what we are to do)—provides the structure for law and covenant in biblical theology (see figure 3.1). Moses himself instructs the people to recognize this pattern. When Israelite parents teach their children the reason for the laws they follow, the parents are to place these in the context of God's saving actions to deliver them from Egypt (Deut 6:20-24). The people already had some idea of what God required of them. They already knew, for example, it was wrong to kill children. The law of Moses is not therefore *entirely* new, though it is the fullest explanation we have in Scripture of what God requires of us. But we also have to read it carefully in the context of the whole Bible. The Mosaic law is not the final word. Some of the laws apply specifically to Israel in a temporary way, and some of them apply in perpetuity. Yet all of it must be understood in relation to Christ himself, who is the goal to which the righteousness of the law pointed (Rom 10:4).

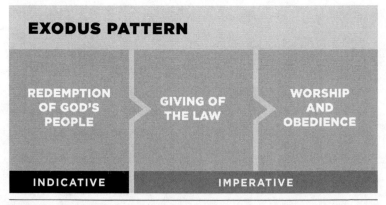

Figure 3.1. The exodus pattern

THE LAW OF MOSES

A new nation. We see something like a declaration of independence for Israel at Mount Sinai in Exodus 19:3-6:

> The LORD called to [Moses] out of the mountain, saying, "Thus you shall say to the house of Jacob, and tell the people of Israel: 'You yourselves have seen what I did to the Egyptians, and how I bore you on eagles' wings and brought you to myself. Now therefore, if you will indeed obey my voice and keep my covenant, you shall be my treasured possession among all peoples, for all the earth is mine; and you shall be to me a kingdom of priests and a holy nation.' These are the words that you shall speak to the people of Israel."

The people of Israel had just come through the crucible of slavery, and God delivered them and gave them their start as a nation. In the Gettysburg

Address, Abraham Lincoln set a vision before a divided country that called the people back to their founding principles. When the people of Israel are delivered from bondage in the exodus, they are given the law of God to teach them what righteousness looks like (based on God's own character) and to return them to the vision God set forth in the beginning with Adam. This is especially clear in the Ten Commandments, which summarize the moral law of God that was written on Adam's heart in the beginning.[2]

The Ten Commandments. The Ten Commandments are first recounted in Exodus 20. Many are familiar with the Ten Commandments in general. But do we know what to do with them? To what degree are they a record of an ancient people's law? And to what degree are they a law for us today? Are some of the laws permanent (like the prohibition against murder), and some temporary (like the Sabbath)?

There is a sense in which the Ten Commandments were given to Moses specifically for the people of Israel. They had just been redeemed from slavery and identified as a holy nation and royal priesthood. They were set apart from other nations. And yet the Ten Commandments are much more than only a law for an ancient people; they are the summary of God's moral law, which is binding on all people in all places at all times.[3] The Ten Commandments articulate what God originally required of Adam and what Israel was called to embody: true righteousness and holiness before the LORD and (for Israel) in the midst of an ungodly world.[4] The Ten Commandments were written by the finger of God on tablets of stone as an abiding testimony and record of the law of God. Israel was also given other laws, and in them we often see the particularity of Israel's situation

---

[2]See especially Turretin, *Inst.* 9.6.1 (1:604); 9.8.7 (1:612); 11.1.22-23 (2:6-7); 11.2.17 (2:12); Bavinck, *RD*, 2:574; see also Irenaeus, *Against Heresies* 4.15.1.

[3]To be sure, there are various views on this issue. Some would see the Ten Commandments as more applicable to the Old Testament era. But the simplest and most satisfying solution, in light of the usage of the Ten Commandments in the New Testament, is that they are a summary of God's moral law that abides still today. I will discuss further reasons for this when I discuss the New Testament. See also G. K. Beale, *A New Testament Biblical Theology: The Unfolding of the Old Testament in the New* (Grand Rapids, MI: Baker Academic, 2011), 871-73; WCF 19.1-2, 5; Turretin, *Inst.* 11.1-3 (2:1-28); Irenaeus, *Against Heresies* 4.16.4.

[4]Compare Sinclair B. Ferguson, *The Whole Christ: Legalism, Antinomianism, and Gospel Assurance—Why the Marrow Controversy Still Matters* (Wheaton, IL: Crossway, 2016), 118-19.

more clearly, but the Ten Commandments uniquely summarize the abiding moral law of God.[5]

As God's covenant people, Israel's descendants were called to walk faithfully before their covenant Lord, reflecting God's character to those around them. This is clear from their call to be a holy nation and royal priesthood; in distinction from the surrounding nations, Israel was called to be a light who reflected the character of their covenant Lord to the surrounding peoples. This perspective is evident in the logic of Deuteronomy 14:1-2:

> You are the sons of the LORD your God. You shall not cut yourselves or make any baldness on your foreheads for the dead. For you are a people holy to the LORD your God, and the LORD has chosen you to be a people for his treasured possession, out of all the peoples who are on the face of the earth.

Israel was to live differently from the surrounding nations. What the people of Israel ate and how they dealt with ritual impurity set them apart from surrounding cultures. Israel served the living God.

Though Israel as a nation was not in the same position as Adam—the people were not offered eternal life on the basis of perfect obedience (for indeed all Israelites were sinners)—Israel was called to a redeemed way of life that mirrored God's created order. They were called to life of faith that resulted in obedience, just as God's covenant people are throughout history. Already in the Old Testament, God's people were called to true obedience from the heart (Deut 10:16).

Threefold dimensions of law: moral, civil, ceremonial. The Ten Commandments summarize the moral law of God, referring to that aspect of the law of God that does not change across covenant administrations. The moral law was binding for Adam, Noah, Abraham, and Moses, and it remains authoritative today. But the Ten Commandments are not the only laws given to Israel. Traditionally, many have referred to the law of Moses as having three divisions: the moral, the civil, and the ceremonial. Civil laws were judicial laws given to Israel as a nation. Ceremonial laws pertained to the sacrificial system of Israel. On this understanding, civil and ceremonial laws are no longer in effect; they were given for a temporary purpose in Israel's history. For example,

---

[5]See Ferguson, *Whole Christ*, 147-51.

the sacrificial system prefigured the coming of Christ, who offered the final sacrifice that never needs to be repeated (Heb 9:26; 10:11-12).

This threefold division of the law, however, is often questioned. Nowhere do we see, for example, that Moses divides the law of God according to moral, civil, and ceremonial distinctions. True enough. Yet some sort of distinction is apparent in Scripture itself.[6] For example, only the Ten Commandments are inscribed on tablets by God and deposited in the ark of the covenant.[7] The Ten Commandments are the first commandments given and are not limited to how to live in the Promised Land.[8] The Ten Commandments do not prescribe specific penalties[9] but are more like the framework for understanding the law as a whole. In these ways, they are different from other portions of the Mosaic law.

In addition, the Old Testament often makes a distinction between moral and ceremonial aspects of God's law. As we will see in the discussion below of the Prophets, God's people often kept the ceremonial aspects of God's law—offering right sacrifices—even while breaking the moral law of God. Outward, ritual obedience is deemed insufficient where there is the lack of true love for God and neighbor.[10] And where there is no kingdom, God's civil law is not the rule of the land (e.g., Esther). Even so, ceremonial and civil laws, while not in effect, continue to instruct us in what God requires, because they reflect the character and will of God. So, while a threefold *division* of the law may segment the law of Moses too sharply, we can at least speak of the threefold *dimensions* of the law.[11]

Understanding the law of God in the context of covenant is crucial if we are to appreciate the purpose of the law and its ongoing relevance today. The people of Israel were already God's covenant people when they received the law; the law was not given that they might *become* God's people on the basis

---

[6]See also the distinctions in Irenaeus, *Against Heresies*, 4.16.4-5.

[7]Ferguson, *Whole Christ*, 150.

[8]Bruce K. Waltke with Charles Yu, *An Old Testament Theology: An Exegetical, Canonical, and Thematic Approach* (Grand Rapids, MI: Zondervan, 2007), 412-14.

[9]See also Richard P. Belcher Jr., *The Fulfillment of the Promises of God: An Explanation of Covenant Theology* (Fearn: Ross-shire: Mentor, 2020), 80.

[10]E.g., 1 Sam 15:22; Hos 6:6; see also Deut 10:16.

[11]Following Ferguson, *Whole Christ*, 143n14.

of obedience. They were to live by faith, and obedience was to flow out of their faith toward God. The law was given to teach the people what God requires and how they ought to live. It was a good and gracious thing for God to give his laws to his people, that they might understand who he is and how to please him. The law was for them—as the moral law continues to be today—a guide for righteous living.

The law as schoolmaster. The law was not only a guide for the people of Israel to live faithfully before their covenant LORD; it also served to instruct, rebuke, train, and even imprison them. This is why the apostle Paul refers to the law as a schoolteacher, or pedagogue (Gal 3:23-25), and Peter describes the law as a yoke that no one was able to bear (Acts 15:10). To understand what Paul and Peter mean, we need to understand that the Mosaic law, as a covenant administration, was temporary and as such served some unique functions. The purity regulations, for example (correlated to the ceremonial law), were constant reminders to Israel of the holiness of God and the need to be holy as well.[12] The law of Moses, as a governing administration over all of life, was temporary; it was not the final word. The law of Moses pointed forward to Christ and showed God's people their need for a deliverer. Problems emerged when God's people lived as though the Mosaic law were the final word from God or if they lived as though the righteousness of the law were to be pursued by works apart from faith (see Rom 9:30-32). Instead, God's covenant people were to live and obey by faith, looking for God's coming deliverer—the seed of the woman.

The Mosaic law, then, showed God's people their need for deliverance. Though the law of Moses was part of the covenant of grace and salvation was freely granted to all who would believe, it also contains a principle of "life by works" that illustrates the path of works to eternal life. A key text is Leviticus 18:5: "You shall therefore keep my statutes and rules; if a person does them, he shall live by them: I am the LORD." This text is used in the New Testament—by both Jesus and Paul—to show the need for perfect obedience if one were to live on the basis of law keeping (e.g., Lk 10:28; Rom 10:5; Gal 3:12). It recalls the original covenant with Adam, where he was offered

---

[12]See also Jay Sklar, *Leviticus: An Introduction and Commentary*, TOTC 3 (Downers Grove, IL: IVP Academic, 2013), 44-49.

eternal life on the basis of perfect obedience. However, for Israel (and indeed, for any natural person living since Adam) to walk this path of "life by law keeping" would be a dead end. If only *perfect* obedience meets the requirements for eternal life, then only two people have a real shot: Adam in his upright, created state (he failed), and the second Adam, Jesus Christ. For anyone else to seek life by law keeping, apart from faith, would be in vain.

This means the Mosaic law is best understood *both* as part of the covenant of grace, *and* as a means to train God's people that they need a deliverer. If God's people obeyed him from the heart, then they would be greatly blessed. They would be fruitful and enjoy long life and great prosperity in the Promised Land. God himself would walk among them and be their God (Lev 26:12). The Promised Land would be a fruitful land of God's presence, like the Garden of Eden. But if the people of Israel rebelled and went their own way, they would face crushing curses. Much more detail about these blessings and curses comes in Deuteronomy, which is perhaps the most important book for understanding the relationship of law and covenant in all the Old Testament.

THE PARADIGM: LOVE, OBEDIENCE, AND SONSHIP IN DEUTERONOMY

Law and covenant in Deuteronomy. Deuteronomy shows quite clearly the way that covenant and law should relate. In fact, Deuteronomy is one of the most important books in all the Bible. It provides the theological foundation for understanding the rest of the Old Testament and is important for understanding the work of Christ in the New Testament. Deuteronomy's importance may be surprising, since Deuteronomy is not blessed with the most exciting name in English (from the Greek for "second law"). By the time readers of the Pentateuch come to Deuteronomy, they may be thinking, *there's more law?*! Deuteronomy is the fourth straight book that contains the Mosaic law; the entire Ten Commandments, first given in Exodus, are even repeated.

Yet Deuteronomy is not a "second law" in the sense that it simply repeats earlier books. Instead, Deuteronomy is a series of sermons that exhorts God's people to covenant faithfulness in light of the redemption he has accomplished

and the words he has given to them.[13] Deuteronomy recounts the final words
of Moses and is the climactic end to the Pentateuch, calling God's people to
renewed obedience before they enter the Promised Land.

In terms of covenant, Deuteronomy exhibits the structure of an ancient
covenant document. It begins by speaking of God's great actions on their
behalf (Deut 1:1–4:43), lays out the stipulations for the people to follow
(Deut 4:44–26:19), offers blessings and curses for obedience and disobedience
(Deut 27:1–30:20), and ensures continuity after Moses (Deut 31:1–34:12).[14]
The book presents God's people with two covenantal options: a blessing or a
curse (Deut 11:26-32; 30:19-20). Moses pleads with the people to choose obedience and life and turn away from disobedience and the horrors of the curses.
In terms of law, Deuteronomy shows us that the law is a blessing. It is not a
burden God's people had to keep to earn God's love; it is the proper response
to the love that God had shown them. The law is given "to guide [Israel] to-
wards the fullest enjoyment of life."[15]

The LORD as covenantal Father. The covenantal contours of Deuteronomy
begin with the God of the covenant. The LORD reveals himself in Deuteronomy
as the fatherly King who has chosen Israel (Deut 4:37; 7:6-7; 10:15). He begot,
fought for, carried, cared for, and disciplined Israel as royal son (Deut 8:5;
14:1-2; 32:6, 18-20, 43).[16] For example, in Deuteronomy 1:30-31 we read, "The
LORD your God who goes before you will himself fight for you, just as he did
for you in Egypt before your eyes, and in the wilderness, where you have seen
how the LORD your God carried you, as a man carries his son, all the way
that you went until you came to this place."

Not only is the LORD the great Father and King of Israel, he is also tender
and loving. In the ancient Near Eastern context of Deuteronomy it was
common for kings to be portrayed as great fathers, but the tenderness of God
in Deuteronomy surpasses what we find in other ancient Near Eastern

---

[13]The four sermons are: 1:1–4:43; 4:44–26:19; 27:1–29:1; 29:2–30:20. I am following Peter C. Craigie,
The Book of Deuteronomy, NICOT (Grand Rapids, MI: Eerdmans, 1976).

[14]Again following Craigie, *Deuteronomy,* 22-24, 67-69.

[15]R. E. Clements, *God's Chosen People: A Theological Interpretation of the Book of Deuteronomy*
(London: SCM, 1968), 58.

[16]Some manuscripts in Deut 32:43 read, "blood of his servants," but the best reading is, "blood of
his children," as the ESV reads.

cultures.[17] The LORD loves Israel as a Father; Israel is called to love him as well. In fact, it would not be going too far to say that Deuteronomy is the book of love *par excellence* in the Old Testament.[18] And the context for Israel's love and obedience is God's prior election and salvation (see Deut 7:6-11). In light of God's actions on their behalf, the people of Israel are to love God.

Israel as covenantal son. As covenantal son—a people redeemed by and in covenant with God (see Ex 4:22-23)—Israel is commanded to love its divine Father (see esp. Deut 8:1-6). This makes sense in the context of the covenant, for in the covenant, love and obedience go hand in hand. In short, to *love God* is to *obey God*. For example, Deuteronomy 11:1 states, "You shall therefore love the LORD your God and keep his charge, his statutes, his rules, and his commandments always." The greatest of all commandments is found in Deuteronomy, which correlates loving God to keeping his commandments: "You shall love the LORD your God with all your heart and with all your soul and with all your might" (Deut 6:5). This love for God certainly includes our emotions, but the surrounding context makes clear that we love God by doing what he commands (Deut 6:1-3, 6-9).

Obedience and love are inseparable.[19] Deuteronomy leaves no room for someone to say, "I love God, but obedience is optional." Practical obedience and true love are required in response to God's gracious acts in history.

This covenantal love and loyalty of a son to a father is the appropriate response to God's election and redemption of Israel. In Deuteronomy the LORD presents a wonderful opportunity to Israel: entrance into and possession of the land promised to Abraham, Isaac, and Jacob. This was an abundant land flowing with milk and honey.[20] More important, the land was a place of God's special presence with the people.[21] God must therefore be worshiped in the right way. Idolatry is deadly and would lead the people away from the

---

[17]See James Earl Harriman, "Our Father in Heaven: The Dimensions of Divine Paternity in Deuteronomy" (PhD diss., The Southern Baptist Theological Seminary, 2005), 223-25.

[18]See, e.g., William L. Moran, "The Ancient Near Eastern Background of the Love of God in Deuteronomy," *CBQ* 25 (1963): 77; Geerhardus Vos, "The Scriptural Doctrine of the Love of God," in *Redemptive History and Biblical Interpretation: The Shorter Writings of Geerhardus Vos*, ed. Richard B. Gaffin Jr. (Phillipsburg, NJ: P&R, 1980), 430-35; Craigie, *Deuteronomy*, 37.

[19]See also Deut 5:10; 7:9; 8:2; 10:12-16; 11:13, 18, 22; 13:3; 19:9; 30:6, 16, 20.

[20]See esp. Deut 4:1-40; 5:16; 6:1-19; 7:12-16; 8:1-10; 11:8-32; 28:1-14.

[21]Deut 9:3; 12:11; 23:14; see also Lev 26:12.

LORD, so the Promised Land must be cleared of all false worship. Eventually the people would have a centralized place of proper worship in the land of God's special presence (Deut 12:1-7). If the people obeyed these (and other) laws, blessings would follow; if they rejected God's law, curses would result.

Though the particular circumstances facing Israel were unique, the principle is consistent with the rest of Scripture. Blessings and life flow from obedience; disobedience leads to cursing and death. Moses sums it up:

> I call heaven and earth to witness against you today, that I have set before you life and death, blessing and curse. Therefore choose life, that you and your offspring may live, loving the LORD your God, obeying his voice and holding fast to him, for he is your life and length of days, that you may dwell in the land that the LORD swore to your fathers, to Abraham, to Isaac, and to Jacob, to give them. (Deut 30:19-20)

The need for an obedient Son of God. Israel as God's son had not yet entered the Promised Land in Deuteronomy, and the permanent possession of it was not a sure thing. In order to experience these blessings, Israel had to maintain covenant loyalty. We are again reminded of the provisional nature of the Mosaic covenant. As wonderful as the promises are, there is a palpable sense of uncertainty and gloom when we reach the end of Deuteronomy. More space is devoted to the curses than to the blessings in Deuteronomy 28. Moses predicts that the people would experience the covenantal curses because of the people's idolatry and rebellion (Deut 30:1-10; 32:19-33). This would be a great tragedy since the words of God were not too hard for them to keep (Deut 30:11-14). The law of Moses—as an administration of the covenant of grace—did not require the people's perfect obedience to walk in faithfulness. Even so, the people would be sinful and fail to remain covenantally loyal.

Despite the people's disobedience, the LORD would remain faithful to his covenant promises, and bring them back after the curse of exile (Deut 4:30; 30:1-10; 32:34-43). He would deliver them from their enemies and fulfill his promise to Abraham to give them a permanent inheritance. Israel is no better than other nations yet is called to be a holy people. The law both directs them as a guide to life, and also imprisons them as a people unable to obey God fully. But the end of the Pentateuch is not the end of the story. If God requires full obedience (which no sinner can realize), and if he grants his people salvation by faith (like Abraham, Gen 15:6), then there must be a way to meet the requirement of full obedience and ensure permanent possession of the Promised Land.

Adam proved to be a disobedient son; Israel would also prove to be a disobedient son. To experience fullness of blessing, there must come one in the mold of both Adam and Israel to meet God's covenantal requirements. Jesus will be the fully obedient covenantal Son of God who brings about the final realization of the promise to Abraham. He will obey in the face of temptation, even quoting Deuteronomy three times showing that he fully trusts in his Father, as the covenant requires. And the good news is that just as Adam's covenantal lawbreaking had consequences for all those in him, so Christ's covenantal obedience benefits all those in him.

CONCLUSION AND APPLICATION

It can be hard to know how to apply the Old Testament today. The ancient world seems so different and the customs so strange that we may wonder what relevance it has for us. It may even seem like the Israelites were saved by keeping God's law.

A right understanding of covenant will go a long way to helping us bridge that gap. Abraham and Moses (and all true covenant members in Israel) were saved by grace through faith in God's provision. The law of Moses does not offer a different way of salvation than the New Testament, but it does present an earlier stage in redemptive history that has not yet flowered to the fullness we see with Christ. In the covenant of grace (which includes the law of Moses) the proper path is always one of faith that yields obedience. And though many of the laws given through Moses had particular application to the nation of Israel, we would be quite at a loss today to know what God requires of us if we did not have the law of Moses.

1. The law of God is multifaceted but remains a guide for righteous living; following the law of God brings blessing. This applies especially to the moral law of God summarized in the Ten Commandments. To be sure, the Ten Commandments show us the standard of God that we cannot

attain perfectly. But they must not for that reason be dismissed or down-played as hypothetical, for they also provide an ongoing guide to how we ought to live. They are practical. The Ten Commandments should be memorized, studied, and prayed over regularly. They must be obeyed.

The prohibitions in the Ten Commandments (most of them are given in the negative)[22] seem to say more about what we are *not* to do than what we are to do. But this would be a misconception; the Ten Commandments also require us positively to pursue righteousness. This anticipates the teaching of Jesus in the Sermon on the Mount (Mt 5:21-48) and the apostle Paul (Eph 4:28-29). God's law not only requires us to avoid certain things but, positively, to do certain things.

The Ten Commandments remain a guide for righteous living in the New Testament era. Without the law of God, we would be greatly impoverished to know how we ought to live today.

Beyond the Ten Commandments, many other laws from the Pen-tateuch reveal God's abiding, moral law. This can take more work to sort out, but it is instructive that Jesus identifies the second great commandment to come from Leviticus 19:18: "you shall love your neighbor as yourself." This is striking, since Leviticus is a book that many today think reflects a moral code that is no longer binding. But the matter is not so simple. For example, the command to leave food for those in need (Lev 19:9-10) is magnanimously exemplified by the selfless actions of Boaz in the book of Ruth (see next chapter), showing us we should care for the poor. This is to love our neighbor as ourselves. Likewise, most of the detailed prohibitions against sexual immorality and unlawful marriages in Leviticus 18 apply rather straightforwardly today, which helps to tease out more fully what "do not commit adultery" entails in the Ten Commandments.[23] It's especially important to reflect God's created order in how we live. In the new covenant the requirement continues for God's people to be holy as he is holy (1 Pet 1:16; see also Lev 11:44-45; 19:2).

---

[22]See also Ferguson, *Whole Christ*, 149.
[23]See Sklar, *Leviticus*, 226-39; see also 172-73; WCF 24.4.

In the end, the law of God is about loving God and our neighbor (Mt 22:37-40), and the Mosaic law shows us how to do this. One might even say that the two great love commandments summarize the Ten Commandments.[24]

In popular culture it's not uncommon to hear of people longing for a life of no rules—pining for a place where there are no Ten Commandments. Yet to throw off the Ten Commandments leads not to joy but to destruction. As a rule for life, the law of God is like railroad tracks.[25] For a train to move efficiently and properly, it needs the rails. This is not a burden; this is how a train was designed to work. Few methods of transportation are as efficient as trains. Yet a train off the rails goes nowhere. Just as trains need the tracks, so the law of God shows us what God desires of us as we live in a covenant relationship with him. The law is like railroad tracks showing us how we are designed to live.

2. Deuteronomy sets forth the proper relationship of love and obedience. God's covenant people had been given God's law and were to obey God from the heart, walking in faith in the context of the covenant. To love God is to obey him.

3. The Mosaic law was not designed to be the final word; it was anticipatory. The particular mode of life, governed by the particularities of the civil and ceremonial aspects of the law, was not designed to be permanent. Paul makes this clear in the New Testament, when he says, "Why then the law? It was added because of transgressions, until the offspring should come to whom the promise had been made, and it was put in place through angels by an intermediary" (Gal 3:19). The law rightly points us to our own sinfulness and to the coming seed of the woman who would undo the curse of Adam.

---

[24]See also Dale C. Allison Jr., "Mark 12:28-31 and the Decalogue," in *The Gospels and the Scriptures of Israel*, ed. Craig A. Evans and W. Richard Stegner, JSNTSup 104 / SSEJC 3 (Sheffield: Sheffield Academic Press, 1994), 270-78.

[25]This illustration does not originate with me. I may have first heard it from Sinclair Ferguson. He has recently used it in *Whole Christ*, 168-69.

If we miss the law's relationship to Christ, then we miss one of the purposes of the law. The law is *not only* given as a guide for righteous living; it also highlights our sin and shows us our need for a Savior (Rom 3:20). The promise to Abraham of an offspring finds ultimate fulfillment in Jesus of Nazareth, born of a virgin, born under the law, who redeemed those under the law (see Gal 4:4-5). Now that Christ has come and obeyed the law perfectly, we have greater freedom from sin and boldness of access to God. Now the Holy Spirit has been poured out more effusively. We therefore ought to be even more holy in our day-to-day living than the Israelites.

SUGGESTED READING

Bavinck, Herman. *The Wonderful Works of God: Instruction in the Christian Religion According to the Reformed Confession*. Translated by Henry Zylstra (1956). With a new introduction by R. Carlton Wynne. Philadelphia: Westminster Seminary Press, 2019.

DeYoung, Kevin. *The Ten Commandments: What They Mean, Why They Matter, and Why We Should Obey Them*. Wheaton, IL: Crossway, 2018.

Ferguson, Sinclair B. *The Whole Christ: Legalism, Antinomianism, and Gospel Assurance—Why the Marrow Controversy Still Matters*. Wheaton, IL: Crossway, 2016.

Poythress, Vern S. *The Shadow of Christ in the Law of Moses*. Phillipsburg, NJ: P&R, 1991.

Chapter Four

THE KINGDOM

DAVID AND HIS DYNASTY

SOMETIMES THE RIGHT LEADER makes all the difference—especially in times of crisis. Good leaders cast a vision and inspire confidence. They understand what's important and what needs to be done. They recognize the challenges. Good leaders benefit those they lead. Nations need good leaders.

Consider the crisis in Europe in the 1930s and 1940s. When Winston Churchill first became prime minister of Great Britain in May 1940, things looked grim. The Nazis were marching through Europe, threatening France and the British troops there. Soon the British would be cornered at Dunkirk. Yet Churchill's punchy oratory engendered optimism and lifted morale. Upon ascending to the premiership, he resolved, "I have nothing to offer but blood, toil, tears and sweat."[1]

Things did not get better right away. But Churchill was resolute: "We shall fight on the beaches, we shall fight on the landing grounds, we shall fight in

---

[1] Andrew Roberts, *Churchill: Walking with Destiny* (New York: Viking, 2018), 526.

the fields and in the streets, we shall fight in the hills; we shall never surrender."[2] It's difficult to overestimate the importance of Churchill's speeches and his presence for wartime morale; these played a key role in the eventual outcome of Allied victory.[3]

Scripture has much to say about leadership, especially the need for a king over God's people. Though God's people were wrong in their motivations for asking for a king (they were rejecting the Lord; see 1 Sam 8:5-9), kingship is consistent with God's design for humanity from the beginning. Adam and Eve are to rule as vice-regents over creation (Gen 1:26-28).[4] The Abrahamic covenant includes the promise of kings (Gen 17:6-8). Jacob prophesies of a king who would come from Judah (Gen 49:10-11). The history of Israel reveals that without a godly king, chaos reigns and the people go their own way. In the previous chapter we saw that after the exodus, Israel entered into a special covenant relationship with the LORD as a new nation. Golden opportunities were before them, but soon the despair of reality set in. The people were stiff-necked and sinful, and soon they were in trouble. They faced opposition in the Promised Land, confronted internal divisions, and suffered from a lack of leadership. The nation was floundering, both in terms of their prosperity and their godliness. Their difficulties were directly correlated to their lack of covenantal obedience. They needed a king.

For many today, being subject to a king is a foreign concept. Contemporary politics are different from those of the ancient Israelites. And yet kingship is incredibly important for understanding God's covenant dealings with his people. A godly king unifies God's people and leads them in righteousness; lack of a godly king leads to grave consequences. If God's people are to walk in obedience to his law, then they need a king to guide them, protect them, and show them the way.

In this chapter I will discuss both the need for and leadup to Israel's kingship (especially in Joshua, Judges, and Ruth) and also the establishment

---

[2]Roberts, *Churchill*, 552.

[3]See Andrew Roberts, *The Storm of War: A New History of the Second World War* (New York: Harper, 2011), 58.

[4]For more on these points, and on the Davidic kingship as a preliminary culmination of God's covenantal promises, see Richard P. Belcher Jr., *The Fulfillment of the Promises of God: An Explanation of Covenant Theology* (Fearn, Ross-Shire: Mentor, 2020), 108-12.

of the Davidic covenant, which brings blessings for God's people and prepares the way for the kingdom of Christ in the New Testament.

GOD'S PEOPLE IN THE PROMISED LAND: CONQUEST, CHAOS, AND CRISIS

Joshua: incomplete conquest. Moses died before entering the Promised Land, and Joshua (Moses' assistant) takes over. Consistent with the principle that covenant blessing goes hand in hand with covenant obedience, Joshua is reminded to obey the commands of the LORD, that they may possess the land (Josh 1:1-9). By the end of Joshua, the people have indeed entered and possessed the Promised Land. They have even defeated many of the Anakim, a race of giants who were a particularly imposing threat and represented evil and opposition to God (Josh 11:21-22; 15:13-14; 21:11; see also Deut 1:28; Num 13:22-33; Judg 1:20).[5] The LORD is faithful to his promises, and his covenant people are beneficiaries of divine favor (Ps 105:43-44; Acts 7:45). Under the capable leadership of Joshua, the Israelites successfully defeat most of their enemies (Josh 10:28–12:24). The LORD is with them to fight for them (Josh 23:3), and he has kept all his promises (see esp. Josh 21:43-45).

Yet in contrast to this entire faithfulness on God's part, the people waver in their commitment to the covenant. The early chapters of Joshua disclose that those who were born after the Israelites left Egypt have never been circumcised (Josh 5:2-9). Though this is rectified (Josh 5:8-9), it is a stark violation of the Abrahamic covenant. Israel fails to conquer Ai because Achan disobeys the LORD (Josh 7). The Israelites foolishly make a covenant with some Hivites (= Gibeonites; Josh 9:7; 11:19), whom Israel was commanded to destroy completely (Josh 9:1-27).[6] And this is just after the people were reminded of all that Moses had told them and after they have renewed their commitment to the covenant (Josh 8:30-35)![7] In contrast to God's command,

---

[5]Moses had defeated some of the Rephaim, also giants, such as Og king of Bashan, whose bed (or possibly coffin) was over thirteen feet long and six feet wide. See further Deut 1:28; 3:11.

[6]See Ex 23:32; Deut 7:2-6; 20:16-18. For discussions on the issues related to "holy war," see Daniel I. Block, *Deuteronomy*, NIVAC (Grand Rapids, MI: Zondervan, 2012), 95-99, 207-8, 476-86; G. K. Beale, *The Morality of God in the Old Testament*, CAHQ (Phillipsburg, NJ: P&R, 2013).

[7]See David M. Howard Jr., *Joshua*, NAC 5 (Nashville: Broadman & Holman, 1998), 226. The people did not ask the Lord for help (Josh 9:14).

many peoples are not entirely driven out,[8] which highlights the danger of idolatry (Josh 23:3-16; see also Ex 23:31-33; Deut 7:1-5; 20:16-18).

The choice before the people at the end of Joshua is clear: would they serve foreign gods, or would they keep covenant with the God who redeemed them from Egypt (Josh 24:14-18, 23)? At the end of his life Joshua is not optimistic; he tells the people they were unable to serve their holy covenant LORD (Josh 24:19-20). The history of Israel proves Joshua correct. The conquest of the Promised Land under Joshua is a mixture of victory and disappointment.

Judges: the chaos of no king. The book of Judges recounts the victories and failure of God's people in the Promised Land. The negative repercussions of Israel's failure to eradicate the local peoples become painfully evident as Israel is continually attacked and oppressed within the covenantal land of God's promise. And in Judges the reason is clear: the people do evil in the eyes of the Lord (Judg 3:7, 12; 4:1; 6:1; 10:6; 13:1). As in Joshua, the people's possession of the Promised Land is both positive and negative. The LORD is with them and raises up judges (something like warlords)[9] who intervene to deliver Israel. But relief from their enemies is often short-lived. God has not forsaken his people, but his people have forsaken him.

We see the failure of leadership with particular clarity in the final judge, Samson. Samson is deeply flawed. He loves a Philistine woman who was right in his own eyes (Judg 14:3, 7). He later visits a prostitute and sleeps with another Philistine woman, Delilah, who would lead to his disgrace (Judg 16:1, 4-20). Yet the LORD remains faithful to deliver his people, even when the deliverer himself is ambivalent about the prospect, and even when the people have not asked for a deliverer. Samson is wrong to cozy up with the enemy, but the LORD uses Samson's lusts to defeat the Philistines (Judg 14:4).[10]

Samson illustrates well the covenant people's ambivalence toward the law of God. On the one hand, Samson appears to retain his confession to the God

---

[8]See Josh 13:13; 15:63; 16:10; 17:12-13, 16-18.

[9]See Bruce K. Waltke with Charles Yu, *An Old Testament Theology: An Exegetical, Canonical, and Thematic Approach* (Grand Rapids, MI: Zondervan, 2007), 588.

[10]In Judg 14:4 it is most likely the LORD (not Samson) who was seeking an opportunity to defeat the Philistines. See the CSB, NIV; Daniel I. Block, *Judges, Ruth*, NAC 6 (Nashville: Broadman & Holman, 1999), 423, 426-27; Dale Ralph Davis, *Judges: Such a Great Salvation* (Fearn, Ross-Shire: Christian Focus, 2000), 167-69.

of Israel.[11] On the other hand, he consistently rejects the law of God. Samson's supernatural strength is not in a magical head of hair. His hair is the sign of his covenantal bond to the God of Israel, representing his commitment to his role as Nazirite deliverer. Samson's disregard for his hair demonstrates his disregard for the law of God; allowing it to be cut is the last straw. Where Samson disregarded the law of God, it proved disastrous for him and for God's people. Only when Samson humbly turns to the LORD in his final hour of need does his strength return (Judg 16:28-30).

Samson is a real deliverer (Judg 15:18; see also Heb 11:32-34), but he is also just the beginning of Israel's deliverance (Judg 13:5).[12] He is not fully committed to the ways of the LORD, and the deliverance he accomplished is therefore only partial.

In Judges 17–21 the disobedience of the people droops to new lows. We find a priest on loan to the highest bidder, a proliferation of idols, murder of an entire town, homosexual advances, fratricide, kidnapping, rape, and dismemberment. These actions are all contrary to the law of God. The people need a king to lead them in righteousness, as Judges repeatedly states: "In those days there was no king in Israel. Everyone did what was right in his own eyes" (Judg 17:6; 21:25; see also Judg 18:1; 19:1). This repeated refrain in Judges shows the people's need for a king, especially in light of the proclivity toward sin. The design for kingship harks back to creation, and Judges also shows us that the sinful people will perish without a king. To walk in the ways of the LORD, the people need a godly king to lead them in righteousness, so that they might experience the blessings of the covenant.

Ruth: royal hope in the midst of crisis. But where will Israel find a king? This is addressed in the book of Ruth, which shows the despondent situation facing God's people during the era of the judges (Ruth 1:1) and provides hope of a coming king.

The Promised Land was supposed to be a place of great blessing and abundance—a land flowing with milk and honey for God's covenant people as they walked according to his ways. Yet in Ruth famine afflicts the Promised Land; even in Bethlehem ("house of bread") there is no bread

---

[11]Waltke, *Old Testament Theology*, 612.
[12]Davis, *Judges*, 157.

(Ruth 1:1). This is not the way it was supposed to be. Naomi's life illustrates this hardship well. Her husband Elimelech ("my God is king") has died, and her two sons bearing the foreboding names Mahlon ("sickly") and Chilion ("frailty") had also died (Ruth 1:3-5).[13] Naomi ("pleasant") views her lot as Mara ("bitter," Ruth 1:20). As these names suggest, things look bleak. The people are not experiencing the abundant covenantal blessings that were offered though Moses.

While Naomi and her daughters-in-law, Orpah and Ruth, were living in Moab, Naomi hears that there is food again in the Promised Land. She exhorts her daughters-in-law to go back to their own people and gods, but Ruth insists on returning with Naomi. She puts away foreign gods and maintains covenant loyalty to the God of Israel (Ruth 1:15-17). Naomi and Ruth thus return to the Promised Land, looking for food. When they arrive, they find more blessing than they anticipated.

Ruth soon goes to gather leftover grain from one of the local fields. In God's providence, this field belongs to Boaz, a righteous man who fears the LORD. Boaz's commitment to the God of Abraham is evident in his greeting to his workers: "The LORD be with you" (Ruth 2:4). If we find a downward spiral of covenant infidelity in Judges, we are reminded with Boaz that there was still a remnant of God's people who loved and obeyed him. Boaz obeys not just the letter of the law, but he understands the spirit of the law's requirement to love your neighbor as yourself (Lev 19:18). He allows Ruth to gather extra grain, in accord with the law of God (Lev 19:9; 23:22; Deut 24:19), and he goes beyond the letter of the law to provide abundantly for Ruth and Naomi (Ruth 2:6-18). Later he deals righteously with Ruth at night when she asks him to be a kinsman redeemer (Ruth 3:9), and he sends her away again with an abundance of food (Ruth 3:10-14). Boaz continues this pattern of selflessness when he agrees to serve as a kinsman redeemer (Ruth 4:9-10).

Boaz is a beacon of light whose actions reflect the true intent of God's law: faithfulness to the God of Israel, manifested in selfless love for others and for their well-being. In spite of the difficult circumstances facing Israel, the

---

[13]See Block, *Judges, Ruth*, 624-25.

covenantal blessings in the book of Ruth proliferate.[14] Boaz provides for Ruth, and Naomi's bitterness is overcome.

Crucially, it's also through Boaz that the LORD provides a king for his people. Judges ends with the despair that the people had no king; Ruth ends with the hopeful anticipation of a coming king. When Boaz marries Ruth, they have a child named Obed, who fathers Jesse, who fathers David the king. Ruth the foreigner (from Moab) becomes the great-grandmother of the king of Israel! The Lord provides for his covenant people.

THE DAVIDIC COVENANT

From Saul to David (1 Samuel). First Samuel recounts the official beginnings of Israel's kingship. In the days of Samuel the prophet, the people cried out for a king (1 Sam 8:1-22; 12:17-18). Though the people's reasoning was wrong—they wanted to be like other nations—their request for a king accorded with the plan of God. Judges showed us that the people needed a king to lead them in righteousness, and already in Deuteronomy Moses had spoken about the laws that God's king should follow (Deut 17:14-20, esp. Deut 17:15).[15] God's people would soon discover that there's a big difference between a godly king and an ungodly king. Samuel makes the consequences clear in his farewell speech:

> And now behold the king whom you have chosen, for whom you have asked; behold, the LORD has set a king over you. If you will fear the LORD and serve him and obey his voice and not rebel against the commandment of the LORD, and *if both you and the king who reigns over you will follow the* LORD *your God, it will be well.* But if you will not obey the voice of the LORD, but rebel against the commandment of the LORD, then the hand of the LORD will be against you and your king. (1 Sam 12:13-15, emphasis added)

Notice the correlation Samuel makes between kingship, obedience, and blessing for God's covenant people.

The first king anointed is Saul son of Kish—an impressive physical specimen (1 Sam 9:1-2). Saul fights valiantly and does much to unite Israel

---

[14]See, e.g., Ruth 2:4, 19-20; 3:10; 4:14.
[15]See also Gen 17:6, 16; 49:10; 1 Sam 10:25.

(see 1 Sam 11:6-11; 14:47-48). Yet overall, Saul proves to be a failure. He offers a prohibited sacrifice (1 Sam 13:8-9). He does not obey the command to wipe out the Amalekites (1 Sam 15:1-31). He makes rash oaths (see 1 Sam 14:24), even swearing to disobey God's law when he consulted with a necromancer (1 Sam 28:10; see also Lev 19:31; 20:27; Deut 18:10-11). Saul is not a man after God's own heart (1 Sam 13:14), and his kingdom would not last (1 Sam 13:13; 15:23, 26-29; 28:17-19). Saul is rejected as king because he disobeys God's word. Saul embodies the dichotomy between sacrifice and obedience (1 Sam 15:22). What God wanted was not external obedience but true obedience deriving from a heart that loved him. The people needed a leader like David.

David is anointed king in 1 Samuel 16:12-13, and he proves to be a king after God's own heart (see 1 Sam 13:14; Acts 13:22). Soon after his anointing, David battles the giant Goliath, the Philistine champion of Gath. It's crucial to note that when David fights Goliath he does not do so as a private individual but as the anointed king of Israel. David fights the battle on behalf of the nation; the victory that he wins benefits the people. In this first major action of the newly anointed king, we see a man who fears the LORD and trusts in his deliverance. Surely David knew about the LORD's victory over giants in previous generations—like Og of the Rephaim and the Anakim.[16] David trusts in the LORD who had proven superior to any wicked forces in the past, and he is not scared of even the most massive opponent from among the uncircumcised. From this point, David is increasingly victorious over God's enemies, especially the Philistines. What Samson began (Judg 13:5), Saul (and Jonathan) continued (1 Sam 14), and David extends (1 Sam 17–18; 2 Sam 5:17-25; 8:1). Under David's kingship, the giants are further eradicated (2 Sam 21:16-22; see also 1 Chron 20:4-8) and the Promised Land comes more securely into the possession of God's covenant people. Having a righteous king provides a means for realizing the blessings God promised to his people (see 2 Sam 8:15). Godly leadership makes a huge difference.

It's also helpful to see David as a new Adam figure. Just as Adam in the beginning was a prophet, priest, and king, so is David. As king, David

---

[16]See Deut 2:20-21; 3:11; Josh 11:21-22; 15:14; Judg 1:20; see also Num 13:33; Deut 9:1-3.

conquers God's enemies and pursues righteousness. As a prophet, David's voice is clearly heard in the Psalms (see Acts 2:30). And there are even priestly adumbrations in David, evident in his wearing a priestly ephod (2 Sam 6:14) and in Psalm 110 in which David speaks of the Melchizedekian priesthood of his son and his Lord.

Promise to David (2 Samuel). Kingship is especially important in the biblical narratives about David. As a king, David proves to be godlier and more effective than Saul. In 2 Samuel David consolidates his rule over all of Israel (2 Sam 2:4, 11; 5:1-5; see also 2 Sam 3:1). David understands that the Lord was establishing David's kingship for the benefit of his people (2 Sam 5:12). Since obedience and blessing go hand in hand, it is a good thing for the people to have a king who walks according to God's law.

Once David's kingship has been established, the Lord enters into a covenant with him. David's victories had accumulated, and the Ark of the Covenant had been brought to Jerusalem. David resolved to build a proper house for the ark and its God. This is the context for God's covenant with David:

> Moreover, the Lord declares to you that the Lord will make you a house. When your days are fulfilled and you lie down with your fathers, I will raise up your offspring after you, who shall come from your body, and I will establish his kingdom. He shall build a house for my name, and I will establish the throne of his kingdom forever. I will be to him a father, and he shall be to me a son. When he commits iniquity, I will discipline him with the rod of men, with the stripes of the sons of men, but my steadfast love will not depart from him, as I took it from Saul, whom I put away from before you. And your house and your kingdom shall be made sure forever before me. Your throne shall be established forever. (2 Sam 7:11-16; see also 1 Chron 17:10-15)

Instead of David building a house for the Lord, the Lord promises to build a house for David. This would be more than a physical house or temple. The Lord promises to build an *everlasting dynasty* for David that would endure well beyond David's own day (Ps 132:11-12; see also Ps 89:3-4). In a world marked by a high degree of uncertainty and turnover of leadership—in a world of constant warring and threat of invasion—this promise of stability of a godly line brings hope and comfort, and the power of God would have to accomplish it. Surely no person could deliver on this promise; it has to be

God's design. From this point on, the kingdom of God—and its king—will remain central in the history of the covenant people.

At the same time, there are conditions to this covenantal promise. If the Davidic dynasty is to succeed, the king must listen to and obey the voice of God. The Davidic covenant assumes and builds on earlier covenantal promises, especially the Mosaic covenant. The king must listen to the laws for the king from Deuteronomy 17 and must walk in integrity according to the law of Moses. The king must not put his trust in horses or his army (Deut 17:16; see also Ps 20:7). He must be a king free from the snare of adultery and the snares to foreign gods that come with it (Deut 17:17; see also Deut 5:21). He must not acquire excessive wealth (Deut 17:17; see also Deut 5:19, 21). He must be committed to the LORD and to his law.

When the king obeys, he could expect blessing for himself and the nation. Yet where he disobeys, there would be punishment. The covenantal curses threatened in Deuteronomy come especially to mind, which include the preeminent curse of exile—expulsion from the Promised Land (which would include the loss of a godly king leading God's people). Even so, the promises of the Davidic covenant mean that God's kingdom will ultimately prevail. There is debate about whether the Davidic covenant is conditional or unconditional. Conditional elements are clearly outlined (2 Sam 7:14), but we should also recognize that, since the Davidic covenant is part of the covenant of grace, the subsequent sinfulness of the Davidic line of kings finds its answer and resolution in Jesus himself—the greater David who rules perfectly. His obedience ensures an everlasting kingdom and the salvation of his people.

Covenant infidelity and kingdom downfall. The downward trajectory of the Davidic dynasty starts with David himself, continues with Solomon, and gets worse from there. These failures can be directly attributed to the kings' disobedience to the law of God. David lusts after and takes Uriah's wife, Bathsheba, to himself. He then seeks to cover his tracks by having Uriah come home to sleep with Bathsheba. But when Uriah refuses, David arranges to have Uriah killed. David breaks at least five of the Ten Commandments in this encounter: he murders, commits adultery, steals, acts dishonestly, and covets another man's wife. His actions are evil in the sight of the LORD (2 Sam 11:27; 12:9). What's more, Uriah is one of David's most trustworthy and capable mighty men (2 Sam 23:39); David's treachery feels eerily like that of Judas in the New Testament. Later David places his trust in his great army, and a terrible plague breaks out against God's people. Though David repents and the people are spared, his actions had already negatively affected his people (2 Sam 24:17). Despite the promise of the Davidic covenant, turmoil, opposition, and rebellion in David's kingdom persist—from Absalom to Adonijah, from Shimei to Sheba.[17]

Things initially look up with David's son Solomon, the paradigm of biblical wisdom. His wisdom and his wealth are known throughout the ancient world (1 Kings 4:29-34; 10:23-25). Solomon builds a proper temple for the LORD (1 Kings 6–8) and leads the kingdom to new heights. Under Solomon, Israel is secure in the Promised Land, and there is great prosperity (1 Kings 4:25). As the LORD was with David, so the LORD is with Solomon. Solomon is reminded of the stipulations of the Davidic covenant: Solomon's kingdom would prosper if he obeyed the LORD, but he if turned aside from God's law, there would be negative consequences (1 Kings 9:3-9).

Solomon does indeed love the LORD and walk in his ways, yet the tug toward idolatry remains, even from his earliest days (1 Kings 3:3). Solomon's departure from the law of the LORD becomes more pronounced in his later years. One of the key problems is Solomon's decision to take many foreign wives. This is not morally neutral; this is contrary to the law of God and causes Solomon's heart to turn away from the LORD (1 Kings 3:1; 11:1-6; see also Deut 17:17). Solomon also amasses gold and horses (1 Kings 10:14-22, 26-29), two other features that were prohibited for the king (Deut 17:16-17). The LORD becomes angry with Solomon because Solomon does not keep the LORD's commandments and he turns his heart away from the true God to serve false gods (1 Kings 11:9-12). Because of this, the LORD would take the kingdom from Solomon's son and divide it. Solomon, the covenantal king, does not follow God's law as he should.

Things get worse with Solomon's son, Rehoboam. During his rule the kingdom splits, and the unity of God's people is severed into Israel in the

---

[17]Absalom and Adonijah were sons of David who sought his throne for themselves. Shimei and Sheba were Benjaminites (i.e., the tribe of King Saul). Shimei cursed David, and Sheba led a rebellion against David.

north and Judah in the south. Both kingdoms suffer from poor leadership. None of the kings of Israel are remembered for doing right in the eyes of the LORD. Judah is blessed with more godly leaders, but not entirely so; some (like Ahaz and Manasseh) even sacrifice their own sons (2 Kings 16:3; 21:6; see also 2 Kings 21:9)! Eventually both kingdoms fall, and the people, already divided, are scattered. There is no king on the throne in Jerusalem, and idolaters rule over the Promised Land. Instead of being free and blessed, the people are enslaved and oppressed.

To understand this history, we need to remember the covenantal choices set before God's people in Deuteronomy. There's a direct correlation between the people's punishment and their failure to walk according to the law of the LORD. Moses warned the people in Deuteronomy that if they did not obey the LORD, then they would be scattered among the nations (Deut 28:15-52). When we read in 2 Kings of the horrors of cannibalism (2 Kings 6:28-29), we can be sure that the people are experiencing the chilling consequences of covenantal disobedience (Deut 28:53-57). Each person bears responsibility, but it starts at the top.

Second Kings helps us understand why Israel went into exile:

> They despised his statutes and his covenant that he made with their fathers and the warnings that he gave them. They went after false idols and became false, and they followed the nations that were around them, concerning whom the LORD had commanded them that they should not do like them. (2 Kings 17:15)

This is exactly what Deuteronomy said would happen if the people disobeyed the stipulations of the covenant (see esp. Deut 28:15-19).

Despite the horrors of the exile, hope remains because of the Davidic covenant. Second Kings ends with King Jechoiachin of Judah being released from prison (2 Kings 25:27-30). He does not return to the Promised Land and the people are still in exile, but this is an indication that the LORD has not forsaken his promise to David; the Davidic dynasty will somehow outlast even the destruction of Jerusalem.

But how would that happen? Hundreds of years would pass, with a few false starts and little progress. It's clear that the people need a new leader: a man after God's own heart, who could bring lasting deliverance. They needed a king greater than David.

DAVIDIC COVENANT AND THE PSALMS

David, though flawed, was the paradigm for what a king should be. He knew the importance of walking according to the commands of God and the blessings that followed that path. He also knew the despair of sin and the traumas of personal tragedy. He may have betrayed Uriah, but he also knew firsthand what it felt like to be betrayed himself (Ps 41:9; 69). Many of these insights are recorded in the Psalms. The Psalms are a treasury of insights into both the Davidic covenant and what it looks like to walk the path of blessing according to the law of God.

The importance of the Davidic covenant in the Psalms. The major voice of the Psalms is David, who writes as a prophet (Acts 2:30), and says much about God's covenantal promises and about the need for God's people to walk according to God's commands. Psalms 1–2 provide an orientation and introduction to the entire Psalter, and Psalm 2 speaks about the royal king who will reign over the nations.[18] Beyond David, other voices recognize the centrality of God's promise to David in the Psalms, such as Ethan the Ezrahite (Ps 89) and the Psalms of Ascent (Ps 120–133, esp. Ps 132). This means that much of the Psalter is particularly pertinent for the Davidic king and the blessings of his kingdom.

The Psalter confirms that the Davidic kingdom is a kingdom that will last forever (Ps 18:50; 132:11-12; see also Ps 89:3-4, 27-29, 34-36; 110:1-4), even expressing hope that the king will be delivered from death (Ps 16:9-11; 18:4-6; 116:3-4; 118:17-18). David rejoices in the LORD's blessing on the king who provides victory over his enemies (Ps 21). God's covenant promises are evident in his faithfulness to his king and his descendants forever (Ps 18:50; see also 2 Sam 22:51).

For the king and the kingdom to prosper the king must walk according to the law of God. Solomon's prayer is for righteousness and wisdom to guide the actions of the king, for the good of the people (Ps 72). After

---

[18]Acts 4:25 identifies David as the author of Psalm 2.

recounting the promise of a lasting Davidic dynasty, Psalm 89 recalls the covenant conditions: David's offspring will be established if they do not forsake the commandments of the LORD (Ps 89:30-32). As we have seen, this is precisely what the kings of Israel and Judah did (Ps 89:38-52). Even so, the LORD's promise to David would not be nullified (Ps 89:33-37). In this way, the covenantal promise to David of a lasting dynasty is built on the prior foundation of the law given to Moses, which provided the guide for righteous living that was to be seen with particular clarity in the leader of God's people.

God's law and God's covenant people. The Psalms are not only for the king. They also cast a vision for what it means to delight in God's law. The Psalms show us that the path of faith is the path of covenantal obedience.

Psalm 1, for example, speaks of the blessing of the one who delights in and walks according to the law of the LORD. This is not the person who simply *knows* what the law says; rather, the one who is blessed is the person who understands the true intent of the law and *does* it. As the Nile River brings life (and civilization with it) to a dry and desert region, so the one who loves the law of the LORD will find it to be life-giving in the midst of an arid world. Psalm 1 does not teach that we are saved by our works but shows us that the path of faith is the path guided by the light of God's law (Ps 19:8; 119:105). It is sweet to the taste (Ps 19:10; 119:103). As David himself reflects:

The law of the LORD is perfect,
        reviving the soul;
the testimony of the LORD is sure,
        making wise the simple;
the precepts of the LORD are right,
        rejoicing the heart;
the commandment of the LORD is pure,
        enlightening the eyes;
the fear of the LORD is clean,
        enduring forever;
the rules of the LORD are true,
        and righteous altogether.

More to be desired are they than gold,
>   even much fine gold;
> sweeter also than honey
>   and drippings of the honeycomb.
> Moreover, by them is your servant warned;
>   in keeping them there is great reward. (Ps 19:7-11)

This is the perspective of someone who knows he is not saved by his own obedience to the law, but that the law nevertheless remains a precious and invaluable guide for life. Psalm 119, which runs to 176 verses, further extols the greatness of God's law. The psalmist loves God's law (Ps 119:47, 97, 113, 127, 140, 163, 165, 167), it protects him and guides him (Ps 119:19, 35, 176). He desires God's law above any earthly good (Ps 119:20, 72, 103, 162). Keeping God's law means life (Ps 119:17, 17, 40, 55, 77, 88, 116, 144, 149, 154, 159).

Clearly there is great reward in keeping the LORD's commands. Elsewhere this is related to the people's possession of the Promised Land. The LORD delivered his people and commanded them to keep his covenant (Ps 111:5-10). In fact, one of the reasons for the people's possession of the Promised Land was so that they might keep the commands of the Lord (Ps 105:43-45). For those who fear the LORD and keep his commands, there is steadfast love that will cascade down to the future (Ps 103:17-18). Those who would truly walk in the commands of the LORD would be greatly blessed in the land he promised to Abraham (Ps 112). God's covenant people are unique among all peoples of the earth, for they have been redeemed and received the special words of God that they are to keep (Ps 147:19-20; see also Deut 7:6-11).

Unfortunately, the history of Israel shows that too often God's people were stiff-necked and disobedient. Whereas blessings in the land and life were promised to those who walked in covenantal faithfulness, curses would accrue where the people neglected the law of God. This is what happened. Israel was a stubborn people who neglected the covenant (Ps 78; 81). Israel doubted God. The people did not drive out the nations but shared in their idolatry; therefore, they were cast out of the land (Ps 78:56-66; 106:34-46). Hope returned with David (Ps 78:67-72), but David was unable to establish the kingdom permanently.

What the LORD desired was not lip service but true obedience from the heart. Too often the problem was a lack of true commitment. Joyful obedience is better than mere sacrifice (Ps 40:6-8; 51:16-17). Too often the people could keep the ceremonial requirements of the law but neglect the true intent of what was required (Ps 50:8-23). Regardless of our public actions, the attitudes and thoughts of our hearts matter a great deal. David knows God hears him because he does not cherish sin in his heart (Ps 66:13-19). David's wisdom remains true today: "All the ways of the LORD are loving and faithful / toward those who keep the demands of his covenant" (Ps 25:10 NIV).

Covenant love and obedience in the Messiah. The Davidic covenant and its emphasis on the true obedience in which God delights also points us to our Savior. Jesus is the king who fully realizes the vision of royal psalms (like Psalm 2; 21; 45; 72; 110), and he's also the one who truly and fully delights in the law of the LORD. It's important that we keep Jesus before our eyes as we read through the Psalms, for it is through Jesus that the dichotomy between sacrifice and obedience will be overcome (see Heb 10:5-7). Jesus is the promised son of David whose obedience surpassed that of David, and whose throne will be established forever. The permanence of this throne is correlated to Jesus' perfect obedience. Jesus held fast to the ways of the covenant—even in the midst of suffering—and was delivered from death, being raised to incorruptible life (see Ps 91:14). This fully obedient, greater Son of David is also able to deliver us.

CONCLUSION AND APPLICATION

We prosper under good leadership. Ancient Israel was no exception. David was a great king and a man after God's own heart. But he also could not bring lasting deliverance. He was a sinner—forgiven, to be sure (Ps 32)—but one whose faults contributed to the weakening of his own kingdom and whose son did not persevere in righteousness. David could not fight the ultimate battle against sin or the devil, who must be cast down for the kingdom to be established (see Jn 12:31; 1 Jn 3:8). It will take the final Son of David to deliver us fully from sin. And this will be done in fulfillment of the promises made in the Davidic covenant. There is much to learn from these portions of the Old Testament.

1. God's covenant people are not inherently better than anyone else. This point was already made in Deuteronomy, but it is abundantly clear as we look at the history of Israel. The tendency toward idolatry was not a problem only for other people; it was a problem for God's people as well. When push came to shove, even God's covenant people, who had his living words, could do shocking and shameful things. This reminds us that possession of God's Word is not enough; we need to imbibe God's Word deeply and obey him from a heart that is truly committed to him.

2. We need a king to lead us in righteousness. Without a king, God's people will be overtaken by enemies and led astray by their own hearts. Regardless of one's political situation today, we all must admit our need for King Jesus who rules and watches over his church, delivers us from Satan and from our own sinfulness, and rewards us for obedience.[19]

   The righteousness of King Jesus also provides a guide for earthly rulers, who ought to reflect his wisdom and justice for the benefit of those they lead. Practically, it's also important to pray for our earthly leaders (1 Tim 2:1-2).

3. God's covenant promises are greater than our sin. The promise of a Davidic dynasty faced many hurdles due to the sinfulness of David's lineage. There were real consequences for disobedience, and many people's lives were turned upside down. Many died. Even so, the LORD made a promise and would fulfill it. This promise was greater than the sins of David, Solomon, or even Manasseh. It did not rest on anyone's inherent worthiness but on the gracious God of the covenant. So also today: in Christ, the LORD is gracious to us and his promises are greater than our sin. Our salvation depends not on what we can do, but on God's actions on our behalf.

4. The way of blessing is the way of obedience to God's law. When the Bible speaks of *blessing* it refers to an all-inclusive vision of happiness and wholeness. It refers to prosperity, fulfillment, and flourishing. To

---

[19]See WLC 45.

many in the world today, these are buzzwords that lead to conclusions that are far removed from David's perspective. Many today think that fulfillment and flourishing to come from seeking one's own interests or being "true to oneself." This is not the biblical perspective. Counter-culturally, the biblical teaching is that obedience to God's law brings true blessing and happiness. There is great reward in keeping God's law, and if we want to have a life that truly blossoms, we must submit our own wills to the God who made us.

Even so, the blessings attending obedience often bring with them hardships as well. We don't yet experience the full range of covenant blessings in this age. This is one way in which the so-called prosperity "gospel," which says we can "have it all now," goes astray. Often those who obey God's law will be mistreated in this world (see Acts 14:22; 1 Pet 4:12-19). The paragons of faith in the Old Testament often did not receive what was promised to them in this age (Heb 11). Likewise, though those who walk the path of faith in this age experience spiritual blessings like forgiveness, adoption, and fellowship with God, we do not yet experience our full inheritance. We therefore must look ahead to the future and the new heavens and the new earth.

5. The greater Son of David rules over an everlasting kingdom as the king over all nations. Already in the Old Testament it's becoming clear that the king of Israel is really the king for all the world. David's great-grandmother was a Moabite woman, and further back in his genealogy was the Canaanite Tamar (see Ruth 4:12). One of his most loyal men was Uriah the Hittite. All three of these people appear in the royal genealogy of Jesus (Mt 1:2-6), which reminds the reader that Gentiles have always had an important role in covenant history.

Further, Jesus is proven to be the king over all the nations in the New Testament through his resurrection from the dead. Through the resurrection, the son of David reigns forever (Acts 2:22-36). The resurrection was the proof of Jesus' innocence and demonstrates that he was fully obedient in every way (Acts 2:24; 13:26-37; Phil 2:8-9; 1 Tim 3:16). In Jesus we see that lasting deliverance truly comes by means of keeping the commandments of God. This one who has been raised from the dead is the Lord over all nations (Act 10:36; Eph 1:20-23). He is not just the new David, but he is also the last Adam—the eschatological man who ushers in the age of the resurrection (Rom 5:12-21; 1 Cor 15:21-22, 45-49).

6. We need to stay vigilant in order to finish life well. One of the tragedies in Old Testament history is the way that those who started off strongly—fully intending to obey the LORD—often fall away from the LORD as years go by. Solomon did not finish well. Israel and Judah did not finish well. Even David, the man after God's own heart, did not finish the race of life strongly. The Bible teaches that those who are truly saved can never lose their salvation—they will persevere to the end. Even so, perseverance is not to be understood passively, but we are called each day actively to believe and move forward by faith.

Solomon's life is a particularly sober warning, given the heights and wisdom he attained.[20] Yet in his later years he turned away from the LORD. Let us learn from Solomon's mistakes and resolve anew each day by grace to follow the path of life and the Savior who leads the way. The apostle Paul reminds us that life is like a race, and we must press on to what lies ahead (Acts 20:24; Phil 3:13-14; 2 Tim 4:7; see also Heb 12:1).

SUGGESTED READING

Davis, Dale Ralph. *2 Samuel: Out of Every Adversity*. Fearn, Ross-Shire: Christian Focus, 1999.

Johnson, Dennis E. *Walking with Jesus Through His Word: Discovering Christ in All the Scriptures*. Phillipsburg, NJ: P&R, 2015.

Rhodes, Jonty. *Covenants Made Simple: Understanding God's Unfolding Promises to His People*. Phillipsburg, NJ: P&R, 2014.

---

[20]See Dale Ralph Davis, *1 Kings: The Wisdom and the Folly* (Fearn, Ross-Shire: Christian Focus, 2002), 111-14.

Chapter Five

THE PROPHETS

REMIND, REPROVE, RENEW

HOME RENOVATION TV SHOWS are as popular as ever. Whether you watch them to get practical ideas or just for entertainment, it doesn't take long to discover that one of the first steps in renovation is demolition. Before someone can get the kitchen they've always dreamed of, they first have to tear out and remove all elements of the old kitchen they don't want. To make a bathroom more functional, all the dated features have to be removed. Sometimes the only way to fix a problem is to rip things out in order to get to the guts of the house. In extreme cases, it may be necessary to tear down an entire house to start anew.

If you saw a house only in the midst of demolition, you probably wouldn't be impressed. You may even wonder how it would ever get put back together to become a livable space. Demolition is a destructive process, but it's also the first step in making things better. Demolition itself is typically not the goal, but it serves the goal of a better place to live.

Home renovation brings to mind the role of the biblical prophets. The Prophets[1] represent a major chunk of the Old Testament (they're more than

---

[1] In this chapter I primarily have in view the Prophets as collections of books: the Major Prophets (Isaiah, Jeremiah, Ezekiel) and the Minor Prophets (Hosea–Malachi). But I will also discuss some

three times longer than Paul's letters) but are often hard to understand. The Prophets speak not only of the destruction that comes to the people because of their disobedience to God's law but also of how God will eventually build them back up in accord with his covenant promises.

Perhaps many think of prophets as those who foretell the future. But that is probably not the best way to think of the biblical prophets. While there is such a thing as predictive prophecy in Scripture, the Prophets are helpfully understood in light of God's covenants and his law. In fact, these are two key emphases of the Prophets. The Prophets consistently remind God's people of God's goodness to them and of their covenantal obligations, and they reprove them for their failure to walk according to the law of God.[2] Yet they also look ahead in hope to the renewal of God's kingdom and the people's renewed obedience. In what follows, I will discuss the Prophets according to these three topics: reminding, reproving, and renewing.

REMINDING GOD'S PEOPLE

To understand the Prophets, we need to understand their historical contexts and the issues they addressed. The Prophets were not so much bringing a new law as calling God's people to faithfulness to the law that they already knew. The Prophets reminded God's people of God's covenants—who God is and what he requires from them. The two most important covenants for understanding the Prophets are the Mosaic and Davidic covenants. This means law and covenant are two of the most important themes for understanding the Prophets.

God's covenants. The Prophets frequently draw attention to God's saving actions both in history and in his special covenantal relationships established with his people. Sometimes the covenants themselves are explicitly mentioned. In Hosea the people are rebuked for breaking the covenant like Adam (Hos 6:7). Sometimes the covenant with Noah seems to be in view (Is 24:5;[3]

---

prophets who appear in Old Testament historical books (sometimes called the "Former Prophets"), especially Elijah and Elisha. I will also discuss Daniel, which is categorized with the "Writings" section of the Hebrew order of the Old Testament canon.

[2]Some prophets address other nations (e.g., Nahum, Obadiah), but my focus is on the prophets who address God's people (i.e., Israel and Judah).

[3]See Brevard S. Childs, *Isaiah: A Commentary*, OTL (Louisville, KY: Westminster John Knox, 2001), 179.

Jer 33:20, 25[4]), and the covenant with Abraham underlies much of the logic of the Prophets.[5] Jacob (who became Israel) is another figure who features in the Prophets' reminders of God's dealings with his people in the past (Is 43:27; Hos 12:2-6). But the covenants with Moses and David—along with the exodus and the establishment of the kingdom—dominate the Prophets. The LORD reminds his people of his saving actions on their behalf and the covenant made through Moses.[6] The LORD also confirms his covenant with David, urging the kings to rule justly. The God of whom the Prophets speak is the God of Adam, Noah, Abraham, Jacob, Moses, and David. He is the same God who has saved his people and given them his law, and who has promised to rule over them by means of the Davidic king forever.[7]

Often the Prophets focus on the covenantal relationship using the father-son relationship that is highlighted especially in Deuteronomy. This relationship highlights both the love that God has for his people and the tragedy of the people's waywardness. Isaiah begins by lamenting the cosmic scandal that the children whom the LORD had reared and raised have rebelled; they had less understanding than beasts of burden (Is 1:2-4). God had graciously redeemed his people and entered into a covenant with them, but the people resisted God and spurned his law. Instead of being obedient children, they were children who acted corruptly.[8] These themes are emphasized throughout the Prophets, echoing the swan song of Moses (Deut 32:4-6, 18-20).

Similarly, one of the most important images in the book of Jeremiah is the father-son relationship,[9] which is particularly used to chastise the people of Israel for their covenantal rebelliousness. In Jeremiah 3:14, 22 the prophet states, "Return, O faithless sons" (my translation). As God's covenantal children, his people should have obeyed his commands, but instead they

---

[4]See Geerhardus Vos, *Biblical Theology: Old and New Testaments* (1948; repr., Edinburgh: Banner of Truth, 1975), 54.

[5]See, e.g., Is 10:22; 29:22; 41:8-10; 48:19; 51:2; Jer 33:26; Ezek 33:24; Hos 1:10; Mic 7:20.

[6]See, e.g., Jer 11:3-5; 34:12-20; Dan 9:4-6, 11-13; Hos 13:4-6; Mic 6:3-5; Hag 2:4-5; Mal 4:4.

[7]See, e.g., Is 9:7; 16:5; 22:22; 37:35; 55:3; Jer 22:1-5; 23:5; 30:9; 33:17-26; Ezek 34:23-24; 37:24-25; Hos 3:5; Amos 9:11; Hag 2:23; Zech 12:7-9; 13:1.

[8]See also Is 30:1, 9; 63:8, 16; 64:8.

[9]Walter Eichrodt, *Theology of the Old Testament*, trans. J. Baker, 2 vols., OTL (London: SCM Press, 1961–67), 1:59.

had forsaken God (see Jer 1:16; 2:13). At the same time, the covenantal love of God is evident in this familial relationship, as we see elsewhere in Jeremiah (Jer 31:9, 20; see also Jer 31:3).

Hosea also speaks of the fatherly love for Israel and of Israel's covenantal duty to respond in loving obedience. "When Israel was a child, I loved him, and out of Egypt I called my son. The more they were called, the more they went away; they kept sacrificing to the Baals and burning offerings to idols" (Hos 11:1-2). In sharp contrast to God's covenantal love, Israel whored after other gods (see Hos 1:2). The prophets often use familial metaphors to drive home their points. In addition to the father-son relationship, marriage is often invoked. Just as it is a great tragedy when adultery defiles the covenant of marriage, so it is a great tragedy when God's people commit spiritual adultery with other gods.[10] (Jer 3:20; Ezek 16; 23; Hos 1–2; Mal 2:10; see also Is 5:1-7). God's covenant people must obey their covenantal God.

God's requirements. God's people were specifically called to obey the law of Moses. The prophets themselves are not actually lawgivers; they apply the law of Moses and call people to covenant faithfulness by walking in the ways they already knew. They remind the people of what God requires of his people, promising blessings for obedience and threatening curses for disobedience. Sometimes the Prophets mention the law of Moses by name, such as in Malachi: "Remember the law of my servant Moses, the statutes and rules that I commanded him at Horeb for all Israel" (Mal 4:4). When the Prophets command God's people to seek the LORD and practice justice and righteousness (e.g., Is 56:1; Amos 2:6-8; 5:24; Mic 6:8; Zeph 2:3; Mal 3:5), they call them back to the guidelines for righteousness and magnanimity in the law of Moses (seen, for example, in Boaz). They often speak of law(s), statutes, commandments, and so forth, which typically also refer to the law of Moses (e.g., Jer 9:13; 16:10-11; Ezek 11:12, 20; Hos 4:6; Amos 2:4; Hab 1:4; see also Mic 6:16).

To understand the Prophets we must understand the law and covenant given through Moses. Though they may not be giving new laws, they do drive home the law in new ways that call for repentance.

---

[10]See Jer 3:20; Ezek 16; 23; Hos 1–2; Mal 2:10; see also Is 5:1-7.

The call to obey the law of Moses and live righteously is especially pertinent to the king of Israel (and Judah). This is another way we see that the Davidic covenant is built on the prior foundation of the Mosaic covenant, as discussed in the previous chapter. Quite often the Prophets critique the king of Israel or Judah for neglecting the law of God. Idolatry was a big problem, and the people would eventually go into exile because of their disobedience. For example, in Jeremiah 22 we read,

> Thus says the LORD: "Go down to the house of the king of Judah and speak there this word, and say, 'Hear the word of the LORD, O king of Judah, who sits on the throne of David, you, and your servants, and your people who enter these gates. Thus says the LORD: Do justice and righteousness, and deliver from the hand of the oppressor him who has been robbed. And do no wrong or violence to the resident alien, the fatherless, and the widow, nor shed innocent blood in this place.'" (Jer 22:1-3)

Many examples of the prophets' confrontations with the kings are found in Old Testament history, such as Nathan's rebuke to David (2 Sam 12), Elijah's opposition to Ahab (1 Kings 17–22), and Isaiah's critique of Ahaz (Is 7–9). In such cases, the king was not the only one in Israel walking waywardly. But he held a special role as the LORD's anointed, and he was called to lead the people in righteousness. Unfortunately, the leaders too often walked in the ways of idolatry (like Jeroboam son of Nebat), which led to the covenantal curse of exile. The king bore acute responsibility for this outcome.

In sum, God's covenant people were to walk in his ways, reflecting the priorities and character of God. They were to be holy as their covenant God is holy. It is a tragedy of the highest order when God's people turn their backs on him in light of the abundant salvation he has provided. He had entered into covenant with his people and graciously given them his law to guide them. Though God's people were to be more holy than other nations, the reality was often otherwise. Israel was even identified as worse than Sodom: whereas Abram intervened on behalf of Sodom if the LORD could find ten righteous people, Jeremiah searched Jerusalem for just *one* righteous person (see Jer 5:1, 14)!

With God's covenantal privilege comes covenantal responsibility—*because* they are God's covenant people, those who disobey will experience the covenantal curses: "You only have I known of all the families of the earth; therefore I will punish you for all your iniquities" (Amos 3:2).

REPROVING GOD'S PEOPLE
FOR COVENANT DISOBEDIENCE

Covenant lawsuits. Because God's people have broken the law of God, the Prophets call them to repentance. Destruction comes when the people disobey. If they want to be spared destruction; if they want to be renewed and experience God's blessing, then they need to turn from their sinfulness and idolatry and turn to the living God. The Prophets make it clear that God has not changed; he is the same God who redeemed his people and gave them his law. When the people experience punishment for their sin, it is because they have turned their backs on God.

A cold glass of orange juice refreshes a dry mouth after a long night's sleep. But if you've ever tasted orange juice immediately after brushing your teeth, it's a completely different experience. What is normally sweet and refreshing becomes bitter and repulsive. You might wonder if the orange juice has turned sour. But the orange juice hasn't changed; your tastes have changed because of the mint of the toothpaste. If you come back later to the same orange juice, it will again taste sweet.

This illustrates the covenant people's experience with God's law. The good salvation of God, and the good words he gave them, had turned out badly for them because of their disobedience. God had not changed; he and his law remained good. God's people experienced curse instead of blessing because they turned their backs on God's law.

A common feature of the Prophets, directed specifically toward God's covenant people for their disobedience to his law, is the covenant lawsuit. In a covenant lawsuit the LORD calls out his people for their iniquities and calls witnesses, such as heaven and earth. We see something similar already with Moses (Deut 31:28-29), but the covenant lawsuit receives more attention in the Prophets. God contends against his people—sometimes calling heaven and earth as witnesses—for forsaking his ways.[11] And this is all the more tragic because of all that God had done for them. These indictments, as we see in Hosea, are clearly raised because the people do not obey the LORD:

> Hear the word of the LORD, O children of Israel,
>> for the LORD has a controversy [i.e., a covenant lawsuit] with the inhabitants of the land.
>
> There is no faithfulness or steadfast love,
>> and no knowledge of God in the land;
>> there is swearing, lying, murder, stealing, and committing adultery;
>> they break all bounds, and bloodshed follows bloodshed.
>
> (Hos 4:1-2; see also Jer 5:1-9)

Though the people know better, their daily wickedness betrays their covenant rebellion. They know the good but call it evil; and the evil they call good (Is 5:20; Mic 3:2).

This explains why Ezekiel speaks of God giving laws that are not good (Ezek 20:25: "Moreover, I gave them statutes that were not good and rules by which they could not have life"). God's law is always good. Why would the prophet speak of his words as bad? The problem is *not* with God's laws. The problem is with God's people who reject his laws and therefore experience the curses of the covenant. Knowing the laws is not enough; God's covenant people must live by these laws. Where God's law is embraced, it is the path of life for those walking in good conscience in covenant with God (Ezek 20:11, 13, 21); where God's law is rejected, it brings death, and in this sense is not good (Ezek 20:25).[12] To walk according to God's law is to live; to reject God's law is to walk the path of destruction.

The dichotomy between obedience and sacrifice. For the Prophets, obeying the law was not merely about external observance. Instead, they help us see the true, spiritual intent of the law of Moses. The problem the Prophets address is typically not the failure to offer right sacrifices but the people's failure to love God and neighbor truly. The Prophets lament the problematic dichotomy between obedience and sacrifice. What God required was not

---

[11]See, e.g., Is 1:2-31; 3:13-15; Jer 2:1–3:5; Hos 4:1-19; 12:2; Mic 6:1-8.
[12]See also Is 48:18-19.

mere ritual but true devotion. Hosea 6:6 captures this disconnect well: "For I desire steadfast love and not sacrifice, / the knowledge of God rather than burnt offerings." Similarly, the prophet Micah states:

> With what shall I come before the LORD,
>   and bow myself before God on high?
> Shall I come before him with burnt offerings,
>   with calves a year old?
> Will the LORD be pleased with thousands of rams,
>   with ten thousands of rivers of oil?
> Shall I give my firstborn for my transgression,
>   the fruit of my body for the sin of my soul?"
> He has told you, O man, what is good;
>   and what does the LORD require of you
> but to do justice, and to love kindness,
>   and to walk humbly with your God?
>   (Mic 6:6-8)[13]

Sacrifices in themselves are not wrong; they were commanded by God. But sacrifices don't work automatically.[14] As we saw in the previous chapter (e.g., with King Saul), it matters a great deal whether one's heart is in the sacrifice or whether someone is simply going through the motions, having no intention to follow God's law. Sacrifice is no substitute for obedience.[15]

Perhaps nowhere is this clearer than with the temple in Jerusalem, which was God's chosen place for his people to offer sacrifices (see Deut 12:5-7, 14; 1 Kings 8). At the same time, God's people should not put their trust in the temple, as if a special building would cover their transgressions. Jeremiah warns the people that their disobedience to the law of God would be punished. The LORD declares that his covenant people will face disaster "because they have not paid attention to my words; / and as for my law, they have rejected it" (Jer 6:19; 8:7-9). Jeremiah delivers a prophetic word in the temple itself,

---

[13]See also Amos 5:21-24.
[14]This further shows the distinctions within the law between the moral and ceremonial aspects, as I discussed in chapter two.
[15]See similarly on true fasting in Is 58:1-14; Zech 7:1-14. See also Heb 11:4.

warning God's people that they must not neglect the LORD and his law, "Thus says the LORD of hosts, the God of Israel: Amend your ways and your deeds, and I will let you dwell in this place. Do not trust in these deceptive words: 'This is the temple of the LORD, the temple of the LORD, the temple of the LORD'" (Jer 7:3-4).

Many of God's people thought they were immune from destruction because of God's covenant promises to David.[16] Yet instead of walking in integrity before the LORD, the people practiced injustice, idolatry, and adultery. They stole, murdered, and swore falsely. They had turned the holy temple of the LORD into a den of armed robbers (Jer 7:5-11).[17] The people should be warned by the example of Shiloh: the place of God's special presence in former days had been wiped out because of the people's disobedience; the same would be true of Jerusalem because of persistent rebellion against God (Jer 7:12-15). Sacrifice is not what God desires above all; he desires obedience:

> For in the day that I brought them out of the land of Egypt, I did not speak to your fathers or command them concerning burnt offerings and sacrifices. But this command I gave them: "Obey my voice, and I will be your God, and you shall be my people. And walk in all the way that I command you, that it may be well with you." (Jer 7:22-23)

This misplaced trust in the temple and its sacrificial system reminds us of the true nature of God's law: it is not a law that deals only (or mainly) with external obedience; the law of God requires true, heart-wrought obedience from God's people. Again, the problem was often not that the people refused to be circumcised. The problem was they were circumcised in flesh only (Jer 4:4; 9:25-26). In other words, *the covenant people often obeyed the outward, physical requirements of God's law, but they did not submit to its true demands.* They heard the word of God with their ears but failed to obey from their hearts (Is 6:9-10). They seemed to love God, but their lives of disobedience betrayed a different reality (Is 5:13; Jer 8:7-9; Hos 4:6). Professing to be wise, they became fools (see Rom 1:22). Destruction and curse would come upon

---

[16]See R. K. Harrison, *Jeremiah and Lamentations: An Introduction and Commentary*, TOTC 21 (Nottingham: Inter-Varsity, 1973), 89.

[17]See also Mic 1:5.

the people because they had broken covenant with God by turning their backs on his law (Jer 9:13-14; 11:10).

In short, the Prophets often critiqued the people for hypocrisy: claiming to love God but lacking true obedience. Many could profess to obey God outwardly; fewer truly obeyed from a renewed heart of faith. The Prophets critique those who honor God with their lips, but their hearts are far from him (Is 29:13). This will be the same problem that Jesus faces when he calls out many religious people in the first century for their hypocrisy (see Mt 15:8-9; Mk 7:6-7). Jesus was not the first to recognize this problem, but he stood in a long line of biblical prophets who critiqued God's covenant people for not living according to the law of God. Already the Prophets recognize that the law is not merely external, but also spiritual, and demands the obedience of the whole person.

The need for justice and mercy. If God's people are reproved and rebuked for their covenantal unfaithfulness, what is the answer? They need to repent, and not just in word only. They need to repent practically, in their daily lives. They need to turn from their sin, turn to the Lord, and amend their ways and deeds (Jer 7:3). If they truly love God, they would also love their neighbor. They would no longer go after false gods or their neighbors' wives (Jer 5:7-8), and they would uphold justice and equity for the weakest among them. They should care for the widow and the orphan.[18] Amos captures what is required memorably: "But let justice roll down like waters, / and righteousness like an ever-flowing stream" (Amos 5:24; see also Amos 5:15). Walking in fellowship with God means walking in the way of obedience set forth by the great King of the covenant (see Lev 26:12; Deut 10:12-13).[19] This is the way of blessing.

These rebukes of the Prophets, showing what obedience really looked like, should not have been news to God's people; this is what the law of God already required. The Lord requires love from his people, not mere ritual (Hos 6:6). God's people should not be cold-hearted toward their neighbors, but they should *love* mercy. The call to love God and neighbor is summed up well in the call to both justice and mercy.

---

[18]E.g., Is 1:17, 23; 9:17; 10:2; Jer 7:6; 22:3; Ezek 22:7; Zech 7:10; Mal 3:5.
[19]See also Kenneth L. Barker and Waylon Bailey, *Micah, Nahum, Habakkuk, Zephaniah*, NAC 20 (Nashville: Broadman & Holman, 1999), 113.

The Prophets call the people to repent from their sin. If the warnings about curses are clear, so are the offers of blessings: the one who turns from his sin will live and be forgiven (Ezek 18:21-32; 33:12-16). The LORD loves those who follow him and walk according to his ways—wherever they may be found (Is 56:6-7)!

Covenant and law in Daniel's prayer. An instructive prayer that speaks of the relationship between covenant and law comes from the prophet Daniel (Dan 9). Daniel knew what Moses and Jeremiah said about the people's exile because of rebellion, but he also knew there was a promise of restoration after seventy years (Dan 9:2; see also Jer 29:10). Since seventy years had passed, Daniel prayed to the God of Israel, recognizing that his people had sinned by turning from his commandments: "O Lord, the great and awesome God, who keeps covenant and steadfast love with those who love him and keep his commandments, we have sinned and done wrong and acted wickedly and rebelled, turning aside from your commandments and rules" (Dan 9:4-5). Daniel prays to the God of Moses, who delivered his law on Sinai and, like Moses, asks for mercy. The people had committed treachery by turning their backs on the law of Moses, and the LORD was righteous in his judgments. The exile that they faced was exactly what God said would happen if they neglected to walk in his ways (Dan 9:6-14). Daniel therefore asks for mercy and forgiveness for his people (Dan 9:15-19).

God's people had consistently rejected his covenant by rejecting his law. Therefore, the curses of the covenant fell on them, including the climactic curse of exile. In response, the LORD said the seventy years of exile would be extended, to seventy *weeks* (Dan 9:24). This mostly likely refers to seventy units of seven *years*.[20]

Renewal and restoration were coming. But not yet.

RENEWAL: KING AND PEOPLE

Given the gloom and doom facing Israel; given the change from seventy years to four hundred ninety years (i.e., seventy weeks of years), was there any hope for God's people? The Prophets seem to say that Israel had always been

---

[20]See, e.g., Joyce G. Baldwin, *Daniel: An Introduction and Commentary*, TOTC 23 (Downers Grove, IL: InterVarsity Press, 1978), 187.

disobedient, and there appears to be no easy fix to this deeply ingrained issue. What then is the answer? Would the people ever be able to please God by their obedience?

The Prophets make it clear that despite the waywardness of God's people, and despite the wickedness that brings the covenant curses, there is hope on the other side of exile. The LORD will not utterly reject his people; he will come to them and intervene on their behalf. Though they don't deserve it, the LORD will be merciful to them and grant them covenant blessings.

Two aspects of the Prophets' hope of renewal are particularly helpful to focus on: the renewal of the king and kingdom (Davidic covenant) and the renewal of the people's obedience (Mosaic covenant). The Prophets anticipate the renewal of the reunified kingdom under a new king like David, and this king will lead God's people in righteousness, as revealed in the law of Moses. This will be the LORD's doing, yet the people will benefit with true redemption and restoration that can never be taken away.

King and kingdom. One of the chief ways the Prophets speak about the renewal of the kingdom is by anticipating a new king like David who would be firmly established on the throne of David. This will lead to blessings for God's people, who would again dwell fruitfully and securely in the land of God's promise. When the nadir of exile overwhelms God's people because of their covenantal rebellion, they lose their land, their king, and their kingdom.

Nevertheless, God's covenant with David is not annulled. The LORD would be faithful to his covenant promise to raise up a son of David to rule on his throne (Is 9:6-7; 33:17; Jer 30:9; 33:19-26; Zech 9:9). Though the house of David be like a fallen tent, it will be rebuilt (Amos 9:11). Consistent with the promises of the Davidic covenant, the future son of David will reign forever (Is 9:7; 55:3). This king would rule in righteousness, wearing it like a belt (Is 11:1-5; 32:1; Jer 23:5-6). This righteous king would usher in the age of covenantal blessings for God's people (Is 11:1-9). Further, under this godly leader the people would be united. No longer would God's people be divided into warring factions. Instead, they would be united under one king (Ezek 34:23-24; 37:24; Hos 1:10-11; Zech 11:7).

The Prophets understand that for the people to be blessed, they must be led by a godly king who leads them in the covenantal ways of their covenant

LORD. For the people to dwell securely and be blessed, they must walk in righteousness. And for the people to be enabled to walk in righteousness—and to be free from spiritual oppression—they need a godly leader.

This is the hope that the Prophets speak of in relation to the coming of a new king like David. When this new king is installed, the people will dwell securely in the land. This was already true in the days of Hezekiah, where Jerusalem was spared because of God's covenant with David (Is 37:35). Yet this was a temporary respite, for Jerusalem would eventually fall. But in coming days, Jerusalem would be fortified against all enemies (Is 2:2-3; 30:19; Mic 4:1-2, 8; Zech 8:7-8). The future Son of David would shepherd his people and protect them (Mic 5:1-6; Zech 10:3-4; 12:7-9). This coming king would rule over a permanent kingdom that would destroy and outlast all other kingdoms (Jer 46:27-28; Dan 2:44; Obad 21). It would be a kingdom over all the earth (Ezek 17:22-24). God's people would experience renewed covenantal blessings, and the LORD himself would be in their midst (Is 30:18-26; Ezek 34:23-31; Zech 2:10-12; 8:8).

These blessings would come to God's people in "the latter days" (e.g., Is 2:2; Dan 2:28; Hos 3:5; Mic 4:1; see also Gen 49:1; Deut 4:30; Joel 2:28). Yet it is unclear precisely when these days would come. Even when the people were restored from exile, the kingdom flutters. For example, Zerubbabel was declared to be the signet ring of the LORD (Hag 2:23). Yet we hear very little of him. Further, we see in Ezra that even when the temple is finally rebuilt, the people still struggle to obey (Ezra 9–10). Sacrifices may have been restored, but sin has not been dealt with sufficiently.

When we come to the end of the Old Testament, it will be unclear when or how this king would come. But it is clear that the people's sinfulness—the reason for the exile—continues to be a major problem. Even so, there is hope for God's people. There is no God like the God of Israel, and he will establish his people in the land in accord with his covenant promises. Despite his people's disobedience,[21] redemption was promised:

> Who is a God like you, pardoning iniquity
> and passing over transgression
> for the remnant of his inheritance?

---

[21]See also Is 59:1-2.

He does not retain his anger forever,
>   because he delights in steadfast love.
He will again have compassion on us;
>   he will tread our iniquities underfoot.
You will cast all our sins
>   into the depths of the sea.
You will show faithfulness to Jacob
>   and steadfast love to Abraham,
as you have sworn to our fathers
>   from the days of old.
>   (Mic 7:18-20)

The people's obedience. To experience true restoration and permanent blessing, the problem of sin has to be addressed. Therefore, the Prophets also anticipate a renewal of the people's obedience. They anticipate a final, end-time cleansing and renewing work of God that will enable his covenant people to walk in his ways. This is the means by which they will experience the lasting, covenant blessings of God. Again we see the principle that blessings and obedience go hand in hand. God's people do not experience the fullness of covenantal blessings *apart from* their obedience, but *as they are* obedient. This does not mean that God's people earn God's favor. They've proven time and time again that they are unworthy. Instead, it is God who casts their sins away and renews them, and it is ultimately God who enables his people to walk in his ways. At the same time, the people have a continued responsibility to walk in God's ways.

The Prophets reveal that the renewal of the people's obedience includes both end-time cleansing and end-time empowering to walk in God's ways.

We start with the prophetic teaching about true cleansing. Though the people had the sacrificial system, which was effective for them in the era in which it was given, it was not *ultimately* possible for the blood of bulls and goats to take away sin (see Heb 10:4). Ezekiel has much to say about a coming day when God would truly cleanse his people, which makes sense because Ezekiel was a priest (Ezek 1:3; see also Ezek 20:40-44). After rebuking God's people for their harlotry, Ezekiel points to the covenant promises of God and speaks of a coming day of atonement for the people's sins (Ezek 16:60-63; see also Jer 33:8). Later Ezekiel speaks of a time when the LORD would vindicate his name by regathering and cleansing his people (Ezek 36:22-25). He goes on to describe the renewal God would grant:

> I will sprinkle clean water on you, and you shall be clean from all your un-cleannesses, and from all your idols I will cleanse you. And I will give you a new heart, and a new spirit I will put within you. And I will remove the heart of stone from your flesh and give you a heart of flesh. And I will put my Spirit within you, and cause you to walk in my statutes and be careful to obey my rules. You shall dwell in the land that I gave to your fathers, and you shall be my people, and I will be your God. And I will deliver you from all your uncleannesses. And I will summon the grain and make it abundant and lay no famine upon you. (Ezek 36:25-29; see also Ezek 11:19-20)

Notice in this passage the close relationship between true cleansing and true obedience. When the LORD cleanses his people, he puts his Spirit in them and causes them to walk in his ways (see Ezek 37:24). And where this happens, covenantal blessings will follow. Jesus most likely had this passage in mind when he spoke to Nicodemus about the need to be born again by water and the Spirit in the Gospel of John (see Jn 3:5).

Jeremiah also says much about new cleansing and obedience, especially in his discussion the coming new covenant (Jer 31:31-34; see also Jer 32:37-41). The new covenant will be better than the Mosaic covenant. It's a covenant that can never be broken. It's a covenant in which the law is written on his people's hearts; God's people truly keep his word. It's a covenant in which all of God's people would truly know him and walk in his ways (see Jer 8:7), and the problem of diverging covenant lines within the covenant community (i.e., Ishmael and Isaac; Esau and Jacob) would be abrogated. All of God's people will be renewed and walk in true obedience. This is what Moses predicted long ago (Deut 30:6). In the new covenant, the vision of a holy God walking among a truly obedient people will be realized.

The new covenant: continuity and discontinuity. The new covenant is clearly a new work of God that the Prophets anticipate. Yet the new covenant also stands in continuity with God's previous covenant dealings with his people. Though the new covenant is a better covenant than the Mosaic

covenant, we must also remember that the Mosaic covenant is an administration of the covenant of grace no less than the new covenant. The new
covenant and the Mosaic covenant are thus not *fundamentally* different. They
do not teach different ways of salvation. This also means that the blessings
they offer to God's people are not entirely different.

We thus must not overemphasize the newness of the new covenant in a
way that severs the continuity between believers in the Old Testament and
believers in the New Testament. When the New Testament authors em-
phasize the true nature of saving faith and true obedience, they often look
to examples from the Old Testament, such as Abraham and David (Rom 4:1-24;
Heb 11:8-19; Jas 2:18-24; see also Acts 4:12; 10:43). If Old Testament believers
truly believed in the covenant promises of God, then they were truly cleansed
from their sin and had renewed, circumcised hearts. Even Old Testament
believers also benefited from the internal, renewing work of the Holy Spirit.
This conclusion follows from understanding the multifaceted work of the
Spirit in applying salvation to God's people. The Spirit, for example, renews
God's people in justification and enables perseverance. Since Old Testament
believers and New Testament believers are justified in the same way (see
Rom 4:1-12), then the Spirit must have already been granted to Abraham
and other true believers in the Old Testament.[22]

This need not, however, deny the newness of the new covenant era in the
New Testament. Old Testament believers' experience of salvation was not
entirely the same as that of New Testament believers. The new covenant era
brings richer fellowship with God, greater liberty, and a fuller outpouring of
the Holy Spirit. This explains why so many New Testament passages seem
to speak of the absolute newness of the Holy Spirit's coming in the new
covenant era (e.g., Jn 7:38-39). Yet as theologians have long understood, these
statements are best taken to speak of a *relative* newness rather than *absolute*
newness.[23] The Spirit had long been at work in God's people, and the promised

---

[22]On the continuity of the Holy Spirit across the ages, see Irenaeus, *Demonstration of the Apostolic
Preaching* 56; Sinclair B. Ferguson, *The Holy Spirit*, CCT (Downers Grove, IL: InterVarsity Press,
1996), 93-94; John Calvin, *Institutes of the Christian Religion*, ed. John T. McNeill, trans. Ford
Lewis Battles, 2 vols., LCC 20-21 (Louisville, KY: Westminster John Knox, 1960), 2.10.23 (1:449);
Turretin, *Inst.* 5.2.10 (1:436); 12.5.6 (2:194); 12.5.15-16 (2:197-98); 12.7.19 (2:223); 12.7.45 (2:231).
[23]Turretin, *Inst.* 3.30.22 (1:308).

new covenant would mark the coming of an even greater day of outpouring of God's Spirit, perfect cleansing, and fuller obedience of God's people. This means we need to understand the difference between what Jesus does in history to accomplish salvation, and how the benefits of what Jesus has accomplished can be applied to both old covenant and new covenant believers. As we will see when we come to the New Testament, this new covenant has been inaugurated, or introduced, with the coming of Christ, but it has not yet been completely fulfilled.

In sum, the age of true restoration would be a day of true cleansing and abundant righteousness for God's people (Dan 9:24). God's covenant people, who had so often turned their backs on their covenant God, would be called sons of the living God (Hos 1:10). They would manifest the obedience and love that was required in God's covenant relationship. But for this to happen, something major would have to intervene. When we turn to the New Testament, we'll see that for God's people to enjoy the fullness of the covenant blessings, for the new covenant to come, the truly obedient Son of God would have to come to deal definitively with the problem of sin.

CONCLUSION AND APPLICATION

The Prophets are best understood as calling God's people back to his covenant and their responsibility to walk in his ways. They warn God's people about the curses that accrue to them when they neglect the law of Moses. They also hold out hope that exile will not be the last word. The LORD will not turn his back on his covenant promises. He will deliver what was promised to Abraham, and to do this he will have to cleanse and renew his people in a definitive way. In the end, the kingdom of Israel will be reestablished, and the Davidic king will reign forever. Though the Prophets ministered thousands of years ago, they remain remarkably relevant today.

1. The Prophets warn against religious hypocrisy. The Prophets critique God's covenant people for obeying God outwardly but not being truly devoted to the LORD. They warn those who trust in the sacrificial system or the temple rather in the God of the covenant. Too often God's people thought that if they did the right religious activities, God would smile

upon them—regardless of their other actions. But this is not the way God's covenant works. The covenant requires sincere loyalty, not just lip service. If God's people truly had obeyed God from the heart as the law requires, they would have loved both God and their neighbor. Instead, God's people loved to serve and honor themselves.

There is an acute danger for God's covenant people who know what they ought to do but who shrug off the responsibility to obedience. This danger continues. The pull of hypocrisy never goes away in this age. All who read the Bible, go to church, and read Christian books need to examine our lives to see if the critiques of the Prophets apply to us. Where they do, we must repent. And where there is repentance there is the opportunity for renewal and life. The path of blessing is also the path of repentance.

2. Sin is a great tragedy, especially among God's covenant people. The Prophets do not downplay sin but point out how dangerous it is and how it leads to covenantal curses. Though we live today on the other side of the exile—Jesus has definitively restored God's people in a way that no one before him ever had—sin continues to be dangerous for God's people. Those in the church easily downplay the importance of sin in the name of grace. God's people in the Old Testament were also the recipients of grace, yet the hardheartedness of so many indicates that they did not fully appreciate the dangers of sin. True experience of grace leads to true obedience.

The situation is not fundamentally different today. Though true believers do not seek their standing before God on the basis of their own, imperfect law keeping, God's law continues to show us what blessings accrue to obedience and what afflictions we should expect for disobedience. We must continue to struggle against sin in the new covenant. Let us not downplay the treasonous nature of sin in the name of grace. We need to listen to and heed the Prophets' warnings against literal and spiritual adultery. We must avoid sin at all costs.

3. The Prophets point us to the importance of God's actions in the past. This includes both God's covenants and the giving of the law. The

Prophets remind God's people of the mercy of God and the power of God to save his people. They also remind us of the true intent of God's law—love, mercy, and justice are more important than mere ritual. In this sense, the Prophets provide an important interpretive guide for understanding the law. We might have the tendency to think that the law is mostly concerned with outward observances. The Prophets show us otherwise. They don't give new laws but interpret and apply the law of Moses to new situations. The law of Moses requires us to love God and treat others the way we want to be treated (see Mt 7:12). Love for God and love for neighbor are two pillars on which hang all the Law and Prophets (Mt 22:37-40).

Do we truly love others, or are we self-absorbed? Do we love justice and mercy? Are we mindful of doing the right thing for the benefit of others, even if it disadvantages us?[24]

4. The Prophets speak of the great work of God in the future when he would restore the people and the kingdom. This would be a day of comfort and consolation, especially for the downtrodden who looked for the redemption of God (Is 40:1-2). Instead of entering into a covenant lawsuit *against* them, he would contend *for* them.[25] God would not abandon his people.

But by the end of the Old Testament, the kingdom is in tatters. Restoration from exile had come, but the restoration is not complete. The prophetic hope looks forward to the reunification of the people under one king. It would be like a valley full of dry bones coming back to life (Ezek 37:11-14). The Davidic dynasty would be like a fallen tent that would be rebuilt (Amos 9:11). But when we reach the beginning of the New Testament, it becomes increasingly clear that no mere person—not even a natural Davidic descendant—is able to bring about the blessings of the Davidic covenant. For the kingdom to be reestablished, for the massive problem of sin to be overcome, God himself must intervene.

---

[24]See also Bruce K. Waltke, *The Book of Proverbs: Chapters 1–15*, NICOT (Grand Rapids, MI: Eerdmans, 2004), 97.

[25]Is 49:25; Jer 50:34; 51:36; Mic 7:9; see also Is 57:16.

As it was in the past, so would it be in the future: true blessing and prosperity go hand in hand with true obedience. But for this to happen, a true king who leads in righteousness must come—and one who is greater than any other son of David. When we turn to the New Testament, we'll see that this is exactly how Jesus is described. He is indeed the promised son of David, but he doesn't come in the way that many expected.

SUGGESTED READING

Coxhead, Steven R. "The Cardionomographic Work of the Spirit in the Old Testament." *WTJ* 79 (2017): 77-95.

LaRondelle, Hans K. *The Israel of God in Prophecy: Principles of Prophetic Interpretation.* Berrien Springs, MI: Andrews University Press, 1983.

Pratt, Richard L., Jr. "Out with the Old and in with the New." *TableTalk* 38.5 (2014): 12-15.

Robertson, O. Palmer. *The Christ of the Prophets.* Phillipsburg, NJ: P&R, 2004.

VanGemeren, Willem A. *Interpreting the Prophetic Word: An Introduction to the Prophetic Literature of the Old Testament.* Grand Rapids, MI: Zondervan, 1990.

Chapter Six

THE MESSIAH AND
HIS WORK ACCOMPLISHED

THE GOSPELS

ANY CHILD WILL TELL YOU. Christmas never seems to come. We wait. And wait. And wait. And still it's only November. We peruse catalogs, websites, and stores for gift ideas. People make lists, hang decorations, and arrange travel plans. We attend Christmas programs. Classic holiday movies play on TV. Anticipation mounts as time slows to a creep. When will the big day come? Christmas Eve seems especially long. You know Christmas is coming, but part of you wonders if it will ever get here.

This feeling isn't limited to children at Christmas; we've all felt it. It could be the first day of school, graduation, a birthday, wedding, or even the start of a big game. We know what it's like to anticipate something that we know is coming but never seems to arrive. When it does, what will it be like?

Such was the situation facing God's people at the dawn of the New Testament. They knew that God had made covenant promises to them and had promised that a king from the line of David would rule forever. They knew the texts that promised God would come to comfort and redeem his people from every oppressor. But the reality seemed much different: they had no king on the throne and hadn't for hundreds of years. The Romans ruled over Jerusalem. God's people had the law of Moses and the Prophets, but the voice of God had grown silent—it had been hundreds of years since any true prophet had spoken for God. The people knew that a new day of salvation and a new law had been promised, but what did that mean? Was it really coming? Would God really deliver them? Did it really matter how they lived in the meantime?

They too were waiting for Christmas—for the coming of God's king to deliver them. They had waited a long time, and it was surely difficult to persevere in faith. The temptations to worldliness and compromise were as strong as ever. From the outside, God's people would have looked un-remarkable. They were apparently just one more people group scattered in various lands. To understand the people's privileged covenantal role and to understand the difference in their God, one would've had to look with the eyes of faith. Israel's God was the God of the whole world. He had done things for them that no other god could ever do. He had delivered them and given them his holy law (see Deut 4:7-8).

Many of God's people steadfastly looked forward in faith to the coming of the Messiah. We see examples in some of the first people we encounter in the Gospels, like Zechariah, Elizabeth, Simeon, Anna, and Mary (Lk 1-2). But many others had turned aside and broken covenant with God. The covenant people had to repent—turn from sin and walk according to the ways of God's law—when the Messiah came. This is the message of both John the Baptist and Jesus himself.

But there's much more to the New Testament than this. When the king comes, he brings a righteousness that far surpasses that of any king—or any person—who had ever lived before him. Jesus, despite his suffering, lived the life of full blessing and true obedience. He shows us the blessed life of Psalm 1: blessing and flourishing come through obedience to the law of God. This is true even though he often suffered and was betrayed by one of his disciples. The Bible continually recalibrates our understanding of blessing in a way that highlights the covenant presence of God with us. As the fully obedient one, Jesus saves us from our sins. At the same time, he shows us what God requires of his people and calls us to a higher standard of holiness in our daily lives.

In this chapter we'll look primarily at how Jesus accomplished salvation. This he did by bearing the curse of sin throughout his life, and climactically on the cross, overcoming this curse in his resurrection to new life. These things he did for us, that we might experience full covenant blessings.

JOHN THE BAPTIST: CALLING THE COVENANT PEOPLE TO COVENANT KEEPING

One of the famous stories from the American Revolution is Paul Revere's ride, memorialized by poet Henry Wadsworth Longfellow. Many know the motto "one if by land, two if by sea," which refers to lanterns that were to be hung in a Boston church tower to signal the arrival of British troops. When Revere saw the signal, he mounted his horse and rode furiously through the region warning the people to prepare: British troops were coming. Revere is remembered as someone who warned the people to be ready.

This historical vignette can help us understand the role of John the Baptist at the beginning of the Gospels. With John comes the return of the prophetic word, and his message is one of warning: the LORD is going to return to his temple. He is like a refiner's fire (Mk 1:2-3; see also Is 40:3; Mal 3:1-4). When he returns, what will he find? God's people must not rest on their pedigree or history. They must repent before the coming of the great day of the LORD. God's people must not presume upon their relationship to Abraham; if God wanted to, he could turn stones into children of Abraham. Instead, John's message is for the people to bear fruit in keeping with repentance (Mt 3:8-10; Lk 3:8-9). These are the words of a prophet.

John calls for repentance, which explains his baptizing ministry. He is signaling that the great end-time cleansing was at hand, promised in texts like Ezekiel 36:25-29. John the Baptist is the necessary forerunner of the Messiah (see Mt 11:11-14; 17:9-13). John baptizes only with water; the Messiah would baptize with the Holy Spirit and fire (Mt 3:11; Mk 1:8; Lk 3:16; Jn 1:33). John's ministry of anticipation signals salvation is near.

It's striking that all four Gospels begin with the ministry of John the Baptist. Isn't it interesting that on the cusp of the great day of salvation, the message is one of activation for the people? They should not sit idly by waiting for God to intervene. Instead, they should actively repent and seek the Lord because the great day is coming (Mt 3:1-3). God's saving actions require repentance and obedience from God's people. Rather than being antithetical, these elements hold together in the context of the covenant. To avoid covenant curses and experience covenant blessings, the people should turn to the Lord.

As the final prophet of the old order, John's message is one of anticipation; he looks forward to Jesus. John doesn't teach that our obedience or repentance can save us, but that God's people should be marked by obedience and repentance. John has a more important role than any other prophet before him because he paves the way directly for Jesus, the Messiah. But when Jesus comes, he vastly outshines John the Baptist (Jn 1:15, 30). John does not consider himself worthy even to untie or carry Jesus' sandals (Mt 3:11; Mk 1:7; Lk 3:16; Jn 1:27). Yet Jesus proves to be the greatest servant of all. Not only is he willing to wash the feet of his disciples (Jn 13:1-20); he is even willing to sacrifice his own life for his friends (Jn 15:13-15).

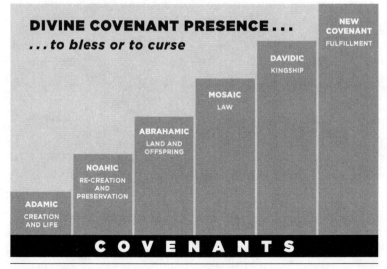

Figure 6.1. Biblical-theological approach to covenants

THE SAVING WORK OF CHRIST IN THE GOSPELS

Birth of the Messiah. The life of Christ—the Messiah—is full of surprises. On the one hand, the coming of the Messiah was amply prophesied in the Old Testament. On the other hand, the way that Jesus fulfilled various prophecies and the unpretentious manner in which he lived did not match the messianic picture that many had envisioned.

This starts with his birth. One might expect the king of Israel, the Son of David, to come from a well-known, prominent family in Judea (where Jerusalem and Bethlehem were). Not so. Jesus instead is conceived by the power of the Holy Spirit in the womb of Mary, an unlikely young woman living in Nazareth who is not yet married. The angel Gabriel announces to Mary that her son "will be great and will be called the Son of the Most High. And the Lord God will give to him the throne of his father David, and he will reign over the house of Jacob forever, and of his kingdom there will be no end" (Lk 1:32-33). The LORD promised David a kingdom that would last forever (e.g., 2 Sam 7:13; see also Ps 89:29). Jesus fulfills this promise of the Davidic covenant. Mary is not only asked to believe she would have a child in a miraculous way; she is also told that this child would rule over the everlasting kingdom!

The Gospels make it clear that Jesus is born as a king. They also make it clear that he is born of a virgin (Is 7:14; see also Mt 1:22-23). The birth of Jesus shows that he comes in fulfillment of the covenant promises of God. He comes as the king from the line of David, born in the city of David (Mt 2:1, 6; Lk 2:4, 11; see also Mic 5:2), though he will grow up in Nazareth (Mt 2:23). He comes as the seed of Abraham (Mt 1:1) and more fundamentally, as the seed of the woman. He is the head of a new humanity, the last Adam, who has come to crush the head of the serpent (Gen 3:15; see also Lk 3:38).

It doesn't take long for the conflict to begin.

The obedient Son of God. Son of God is one of the most important categories for understanding the person and work of Christ in the Gospels. As Son of God, Jesus is the second person of the Trinity. Yet Jesus also fulfills various Old Testament categories of sonship. As we have seen, as Son of God, Jesus is Son of David. He is therefore truly descended from David and heir to the Davidic throne (Mt 1:1-17; Lk 3:23-38). Further, as Son of God Jesus sums up and represents the nation of Israel, which was often known as God's son. This is clear when Matthew identifies Jesus as son of Abraham (Mt 1:1), and in the temptation accounts where Jesus relives Israel's experiences in the wilderness (Mt 4:1-11; Lk 4:1-13). Further, as Son of God Jesus is a new Adam (Lk 3:38). In all these ways—as the Son greater than Adam, Israel, and David— Jesus proves to be the true covenantal Son of God, obeying God fully, which results in our salvation.

How does he do this? Jesus' public ministry commences with his baptism by John the Baptist. By submitting to John's baptism of repentance for the forgiveness of sins, Jesus responds appropriately to the prophetic call of repentance and shows solidarity with the people he came to save. John recognizes that Jesus has no need for his baptism, but it is fitting for Jesus to participate in it as part of his task to fulfill all righteousness (Mt 3:13-15).[1] Jesus is not a sinner, but he came to save sinners. Jesus is baptized as a representative who acts on behalf of his people.

When Jesus is baptized, the heavens are opened and the voice of God returns, identifying Jesus as the well-pleasing Son of God (Mt 3:17; Mk 1:11; Lk 3:22). The Spirit descends on Jesus as a dove, perhaps recalling the original creation (when the Spirit hovered like a bird, Gen 1:2), the new creation with Noah (Gen 8:8-12), and the new creation of the exodus in which the LORD overshadowed his covenant people (Deut 32:11). Immediately after this, Jesus is led into the wilderness to be tempted by the devil (Mt 4:1; Mk 1:13; Lk 4:1-2).

This is a crucial moment in world history. The incarnate Son of God, full of the power of the Holy Spirit, enters the wilderness and faces off with the devil. In the initial conflict of Jesus' public ministry—at the very outset—Jesus delivers the devil a crushing blow, the effects of which will be evident throughout the ensuing ministry of Jesus.

In the wilderness Jesus embodies perfect covenant love and obedience. We see what an obedient son should be, in contrast to both Israel and Adam. The contrast with Israel is clear in Matthew and Luke, where Jesus quotes from Deuteronomy three times, recalling Israel's wilderness wanderings as son of God. When the people of Israel were called out of Egypt in the exodus, they were called a son of God (Ex 4:22-23), and as the LORD's beloved, covenantal

---

[1]See also Geerhardus Vos, *Biblical Theology: Old and New Testaments* (1948; repr., Edinburgh: Banner of Truth, 1975), 320.

son, Israel was nourished and cared for in the wilderness (see Deut 1:31). As the son of God, the people were also tested, in order that God might know what was in their heart (Deut 8:2)—did they truly love God, or would they turn aside when things got hard? By and large, Israel failed and proved to be a disobedient son of God. Because of this, they experienced covenant curses rather than blessings. In contrast, Jesus obeys. He does not cave to temptation. Jesus recognizes that the Son of God must keep the commandments of God (Deut 8:5-6). To love is to obey. In response to the devil's misuse of Psalm 91 (Mt 4:5-6; Lk 4:9-11), Jesus knows that instead of testing God, the one who trusts in God will have authority over scorpions and serpents (Ps 91:13-14).[2]

Even more fundamentally, Jesus' obedience in the wilderness overcomes the sin of Adam. Though Israel was called to be a light to the surrounding nations, Israel was not called to save the world by perfect obedience; Israel was a nation of sinners. On the other hand, Adam in his created state was offered the goal of eternal life on the condition of perfect obedience. Adam disobeyed the law of God and brought death; Jesus obeys the law of God perfectly and brings life.

Allusions to Adam are most likely present in Mark's temptation account, which is much briefer than Matthew's or Luke's: "And [Jesus] was in the wilderness forty days, being tempted by Satan. And he was with the wild animals, and the angels were ministering to him" (Mk 1:13). After Adam's fall, wild animals have been a threat and are even indicative of covenantal curses (Lev 26:22; Deut 32:24). Yet the animals do not overcome Jesus; Jesus' obedience yields peace that was forfeited by Adam's fall. This shows us that new creation has come as Jesus overcomes Adam's sin.

Luke's temptation account also identifies Jesus as the new Adam. After Jesus is baptized as Son of God (Lk 3:21-22), Luke's genealogy traces Jesus back to Adam, who is Son of God (Lk 3:38). Jesus is then tempted as Son of God in the wilderness (Lk 4:1-13). The structure of Luke's Gospel helps us see that Jesus' divine sonship not only recalls Israel's sonship, but also Adam's sonship: to be Son of God for Luke means being like Adam (Lk 3:38), Israel (Lk 4:1-13), and even David (Lk 1:31-33)—but better. Luke has a rich covenantal

---

[2]See Brandon D. Crowe, *The Last Adam: A Theology of the Obedient Life of Jesus in the Gospels* (Grand Rapids, MI: Baker Academic, 2017), 159-61.

Christology that draws liberally from the Old Testament, showing how Jesus fulfills the covenants made with Adam, Moses, and David. And at every turn, Jesus is fully obedient.

From the beginning the Gospels set us up to understand that Jesus is the fully obedient Savior who rescues us from our sins. In contrast to previous deliverers who brought only partial deliverance (think, for example, of Samson), Jesus brings full deliverance, and this is coordinate with his entire devotion to the will of God. Jesus always does what pleases his Father.

The king of the kingdom. After Jesus obeys in the face of temptation, he proclaims the coming of the kingdom of God: "The time is fulfilled, and the kingdom of God is at hand; repent and believe in the gospel" (Mk 1:15). As Son of God, Jesus is the king of the kingdom. He is the righteous king anticipated in the Prophets who will reunify the people and lead them to lasting peace and prosperity.

Yet this kingdom comes in a surprising way. The kingdom does not come all at once but with an unassuming beginning. Neither does Jesus come in the way that many expected the king to come. Instead of marching into Jerusalem with an army, Jesus spends much of his time traveling the countryside in relative obscurity. Is this what was expected for the king from the line of David? After all, David defeated many armies in battle. But Jesus' battles look different. Yet when Jesus does choose to enter Jerusalem as the king, the Bible tells us there should be no doubt that Jesus is indeed the true king from the throne of David (see Zech 9:9).

From the beginning of his ministry, Jesus speaks about the kingdom of God (which is also to speak of the gospel, Mk 1:14-15). Participation in the kingdom requires repentance, for it is a kingdom of righteousness. And though Jesus announces the nearness of the kingdom at the outset of his ministry, the kingdom had not yet come in fullness. Instead, the kingdom comes like a mustard seed: it starts obscurely and unimpressively but eventually grows into a great tree that provides shade for all the birds of the world (Mk 4:30-32; see also Ezek 17:23).

The parable of the mustard seed also shows us that the kingdom comes in stages; it doesn't appear in its fullness all at once. Early on the kingdom has come near (Mt 4:17), but as Jesus' ministry expands, through the power of the Spirit, the kingdom takes root and its influence is more apparent (Mt 12:28). The kingdom spreads even further after Jesus' resurrection and ascension and become a worldwide movement. Even so, we await the consummation of the kingdom when Jesus returns.

As the king of the kingdom, Jesus also calls a community centered around himself. It is highly significant that Jesus calls *twelve* disciples. These twelve disciples represent the twelve tribes of New Israel. Just as there were twelve sons of Jacob, and thus twelve tribes of Israel who were the foundation for the nation of Israel (see Gen 49:28), now Jesus calls twelve apostles who will be the core of a new Israel. These apostles, however, are even greater than the twelve tribes because they represent the fullness of the kingdom that Christ brings (see Mt 19:28; Lk 22:30). This is also a kingly act, for the one who calls the disciples calls them to the kingdom. Jesus gives this new covenant community a name: the church (Mt 16:18; see also Mt 18:17). Jesus speaks more explicitly about the church after the disciples recognize him as the *Christ*—the king of God's kingdom (see esp. Mt 16:16; see also Mk 8:29; Lk 9:20).

Even so, though Peter recognizes Jesus is the king, the disciples still don't understand the sort of king he is. After Peter confesses Jesus as the Christ, Jesus begins to teach the disciples of his coming suffering, death, and resurrection. This is the sort of king he is; this is how the kingdom will come. We receive the blessing because he bore the curse.

As king, Jesus is also the Servant spoken of by the prophet Isaiah. The Gospels often identify Jesus as the Servant, such at his baptism, where the Father's good pleasure in Jesus likely echoes the servant from Isaiah 42:1 (see also Mt 3:17; Mk 1:11; Lk 3:22). Isaiah 42 is also quoted at length in Matthew 12:18-21:

> Behold, my servant whom I have chosen,
>   my beloved with whom my soul is well pleased.
> I will put my Spirit upon him,
>   and he will proclaim justice to the Gentiles.
> He will not quarrel or cry aloud,
>   nor will anyone hear his voice in the streets;
> a bruised reed he will not break,

and a smoldering wick he will not quench,

until he brings justice to victory;

and in his name the Gentiles will hope. (Mt 12:18-21)

Immediately following this passage Matthew speaks of the way that Jesus brings the kingdom by means of his Spirit-empowered obedience (Mt 12:22-32). Jesus is the Servant, filled with the Spirit, who does the will of God entirely. By the power of the Spirit Jesus casts out demons and brings the kingdom, showing that he is the true son of David (Mt 12:23).

Jesus is also identified as the Servant on the Mount of Transfiguration (Mt 17:5; Lk 9:35). In the transfiguration Jesus is again identified as the well-pleasing Son of God and is the one to whom we must listen (Mt 17:5; Mk 9:7; Lk 9:35). The radiant brilliance of Jesus on the Mount of Transfiguration also reveals Jesus' *divinity*. Moses' face shone with reflected glory when he spoke with God in the Old Testament; Jesus' radiance is a of a different sort. It is not reflected glory but the inherent glory of the Son of God.

Yet this divine servant king has to suffer and die. The disciples don't understand how this could be. How could the Son of the living God face death (see Mt 16:16)? The transfiguration provides confirmation that even as Jesus faces the suffering of the cross, he remains the fully pleasing, obedient Son of God.[3] His suffering is not punishment for disobedience or a lack of faith. Instead, his suffering is part of his obedience as he will give his life as payment for sin. Jesus is not just a servant; he is the *Suffering Servant*.

THE DEATH AND RESURRECTION OF CHRIST

Jesus teaches that the path of discipleship is the path of obedience (see next chapter). But no descendant of Adam is able by obedience to gain life. We all fall short. We are in desperate need of a Savior.

That's why it's such good news that Jesus lived a perfect life as our representative. Jesus lives the life that we cannot and bore the curse and penalty for our sins. This is true throughout his life but is especially clear on the cross. In this section we'll look at Jesus' sacrifice and how the new covenant is sealed

---

[3]The transfiguration occurs just after Jesus' first clear prediction of his death and resurrection in the Gospels (Mt 16:21-28; Mk 8:31-38; Lk 9:21-27).

in his blood. By his death and resurrection, he seals his work and ensures a kingdom in which blessings last forever.

Obedience and salvation. One of the major critiques of the Prophets was the dichotomy between obedience and sacrifice—the people often offered sacrifices while lacking true obedience. The answer to this selective obedience to God's law comes with Christ, who is perfectly devoted to God and offers himself as the final sacrifice.

The Gospel of Matthew is full of Old Testament quotations, but the only text he quotes twice is Hosea 6:6: "I desire mercy, and not sacrifice" (Mt 9:13; 12:7). The term translated in the New Testament *mercy* is the Old Testament term often used for covenant love (*ḥesed*).[4] It refers both to the LORD's faithfulness to the covenant[5] and to the people's need to demonstrate covenant loyalty to the LORD (and to their neighbors).[6] Whereas too often God's people neglected to show true mercy, Jesus embodies the merciful love that God requires. In Jesus there is no dichotomy between obedience and sacrifice; Jesus is not like those who honored God only with their lips while their hearts were far from God (Is 29:13; Mt 15:7-9). Jesus is no hypocrite. Jesus lives true covenant love. He does all that God requires, perfectly, and bears the penalty for sin in his own body. Jesus is the lamb of God who takes away the sin of the world (Jn 1:29). He brings about the end-time expectation of cleansing that Ezekiel prophesied and John the Baptist prefigured (see Jn 3:1-21, esp. Jn 3:5).

Blood of the covenant. All four Gospel writers devote a great deal of space to the death of Christ. Jesus' crucifixion is his climactic act of obedience, and it serves as the final sacrifice to deal with sin. During the week before his death, Jesus is often at the temple in Jerusalem, and he provides a prophetic critique against the temple. The temple was the place of sacrifice. More than that, it was the special place of God's presence that provided a focal point for the life of Israel. The covenant promise that God would be with his people is focused in a special way in the temple. Yet Jesus shows us that the temple

---

[4]In this paragraph I draw from Crowe, *Last Adam*, 172-78.
[5]Ex 15:13; 20:6; 34:6-7; Num 14:18-19; Deut 5:10; 7:9, 12; 2 Sam 7:15; 22:51; 1 Kings 8:23; 2 Chron 6:14; Ps 6:4; 18:50; 23:6; 40:11; 89:33; Is 54:8, 10; Jer 9:24; 31:3; 32:18; 33:11; Hosea 2:19; Joel 2:13; Jon 4:2; Mic 7:18, 20.
[6]Prov 19:22; 20:28; Hos 4:1-2; 6:4-11; 11:12–12:14; Mic 6:8; Zech 7:9.

building was not permanent. Instead, it anticipated the final temple, who is Christ himself. Jesus is the means by which sin is dealt with; Jesus is the focal point of God's communion with his people. Jesus himself is the realization of God's presence with us—he is Immanuel (Mt 1:23; 28:20).

The temple itself was not the problem, but it was wrong to put one's hope in the temple when God was doing a new thing. In chapter five we saw how Jeremiah critiqued the people of Jerusalem for putting their trust in outward rites and symbols rather than in God himself. Jeremiah critiques the people for trusting in the temple while they walked astray and turned their backs on God (Jer 7). Jesus picks up these words of Jeremiah in the final week of his life to point out the foolishness of trusting in the temple when the substance to which the temple pointed stood in their midst, "And he was teaching them and saying to them, 'Is it not written, "My house shall be called a house of prayer for all the nations" [Is 56:7]? But you have made it a den of robbers'" (Mk 11:17; see also Jer 7:11).

Here Jesus critiques the people for buying and selling in the temple precincts. Yet his critique is about more than buying and selling: he critiques those who cling to a mode of addressing sin that was backward-looking rather than forward-looking. Like Jeremiah, Jesus critiques the people for trusting in external rites and symbols for forgiveness while not walking according to what God truly desires. This is an even more egregious sin in Jesus' day, given that the goal to which the entire sacrificial system pointed had come. As the final temple, Jesus is the final sacrifice. He is the Good Shepherd who is also the lamb of God, and thus lays down his life for his sheep (Jn 10:11).

Jesus speaks directly about the purpose of his death. After Peter confesses Jesus as the Christ, Jesus states succinctly the nature of his sacrifice as his public ministry neared its end: "For even the Son of Man came not to be served but to serve, and to give his life as a ransom for many" (Mk 10:45; see also Mt 20:28). Jesus' death is not an accident; nor is it simply the exemplary death of a martyr. Jesus intentionally lays down his life as a ransom—a means of redemption—for his people. His death is substitutionary, given "on behalf of" the many he came to save. Jesus came not to be served, but to serve. He is the Suffering Servant who served to the point of laying down his own life (see Is 53:10-12). As the perfectly obedient Son of God—truly man and truly God—Jesus is uniquely able to offer his own life as a sacrifice for human sin and rise again overcoming death and granting new life.

On the last night of his life, Jesus again states clearly the purpose for his death. At the last supper Jesus takes bread, breaks it, and states that it is his body, given for the disciples (Lk 22:19). After dinner he takes a cup of wine and gives it to his disciples to drink, stating, "for this is my blood of the covenant, which is poured out for many for the forgiveness of sins" (Mt 26:28). Blood was a familiar part of covenant life. When Moses mediated God's covenant at Sinai the people were sprinkled with blood (Ex 24:6-8). But here something is different. Jesus doesn't speak of the blood of the covenant as the blood of oxen, bulls, or goats. Instead, the blood of the covenant is *his own blood*. Jesus' blood is qualitatively different from the blood of sacrificial animals. His blood is the blood of the perfect, covenant-keeping God-man. By his blood Jesus is able to deal definitively with sin.

In the introduction I noted the legendary quest for the holy grail—the fabled cup of eternal life that was sought by (among others) Indiana Jones. Supposedly, the one who drank from that cup would receive eternal life. Though it makes for good entertainment, that approach is superstitious. There's nothing about the cup itself that brings eternal life. It's just a cup. Nor is there anything special about the wine itself. It's just wine. Eternal life is not granted automatically to anyone who drinks from a special cup, nor is eternal life granted automatically to those who participate in the Lord's Supper. The Bible is full of examples of covenant members who participate in outward rites but whose hearts are not right before God.

And yet the cup from the Last Supper does point us to the means of eternal life. Life is not in the cup itself or in magical wine, but in what the cup signifies and seals: the blood of Christ—the blood of the covenant—poured out for the forgiveness of sins. We do not participate in this cup in a perfunctory or mechanical manner. Instead, the cup of Christ calls for faith in the Christ whose death is represented by the cup. To partake of the Lord's Supper is to look back to what Christ has done, look presently to Christ as the object of our faith, and look ahead to the return of Christ when the kingdom will be consummated (see Mt 26:29; Mk 14:25; Lk 22:18; 1 Cor 11:23-26). Eternal life comes by abiding in Christ by faith—the one who gave his life that we might live (see Jn 6:29, 48-58; 15:1-11).

The Last Supper points us to the sacrifice of Christ for us. He is given in our place as a ransom. Deuteronomy teaches that a person hanged on a tree is cursed (Deut 21:23). This highlights the way that Christ's death bears the curse for us as a substitutionary representative (see Acts 13:29; Gal 3:13). Though Jesus is the perfectly obedient Son, he bears the penalty for disobedience. He is sent to the cross as an innocent man (Lk 23:47; Jn 19:6). Yet even in this cursedness, Jesus dies as the king (Jn 19:14-22)—the righteous last Adam whose work destroys the disobedience of the first Adam.

Resurrection and new life. If Jesus only died on the cross, then salvation would not be complete. If the Gospels ended with the death of Christ, they would be unresolved narratives that would seem to vindicate the opponents of Jesus and cast doubt on the message and work of Christ.[7] But thankfully that is not how the Gospels end. Instead, the Gospels end with the resurrection of Jesus.[8] The resurrection proves that Jesus was right and that his sacrifice truly brings forgiveness of sins and justification—a right standing before God. In his resurrection Jesus is vindicated and his innocence is declared for all to see. In his resurrection Jesus moves from the curse-bearer as our mediator to the one who is blessed of his Father.[9]

The resurrection is a world-changing event. Though the Gospel writers don't devote much attention to teasing out the implications of Jesus' resurrection, this will occupy the teaching of much of the rest of the New Testament. If Jesus is Lord over all by means of his resurrection, how then should we live? We will consider this further in subsequent chapters.

As we conclude this chapter, it may be helpful to compare and contrast Jesus' saving work to one of the previous redeemers we have encountered in the history of redemption: Samson. Samson was a deliverer of God's people,

---

[7]Crowe, *Last Adam*, 192-97; see also W. D. Davies and Dale C. Allison Jr., *A Critical and Exegetical Commentary on the Gospel According to St. Matthew*. 3 vols. ICC (Edinburgh: T&T Clark, 1988–97), 3:673.

[8]There is debate about where the Gospel of Mark ends. Yet even if Mark ends at 16:8, the resurrection of Jesus is not in doubt (Mk 8:31; 9:9, 31; 10:34; 16:6-7).

[9]Geerhardus Vos, *Reformed Dogmatics*, ed. and trans. Richard B. Gaffin Jr., 5 vols. (Bellingham, WA: Lexham Press, 2012–16), 3:219.

but his purposes were often not aligned with God's (Judg 14:4). Samson also saved God's people by sacrificing his own life. By his death he did more to defeat the enemies of God's people than he did during his life (Judg 16:30). Yet Samson perished when the temple at Gaza was destroyed.

Jesus is a better Redeemer than Samson. Whereas Samson was often callous to the law of God and yielded to temptation, Jesus delighted in God's law and obeyed in the face of temptation. Samson selfishly and violently retaliated for personal wrongs; Jesus taught and modeled what it means to turn the other cheek. Unlike Samson, Jesus was fully devoted to the will of God. And unlike Samson, Jesus not only gave his life for temporary deliverance but rose again to new life, bringing forgiveness, justification, and resurrection life for his people (see Acts 13:36-39). Jesus rose again as the perfectly obedient king who reigns over an everlasting kingdom. He rose again as the final temple, from whom comes the living waters of life.[10]

To understand more fully the implications this has for us today, we must look to the rest of the New Testament. There we will again see the familiar pattern: blessed life in God's kingdom means obedience to God's covenant commands. Though much changes when Jesus comes, this paradigm does not fundamentally change.

CONCLUSION AND APPLICATION

The work of Christ in the Gospels is richly multifaceted. Jesus does so many wonderful things that his life can be difficult to summarize in short scope (see Jn 21:25). In this chapter I have sketched the way that Jesus fulfills God's covenantal designs for humanity by perfectly obeying God. He is greater than Adam, Noah, Abraham, Moses, Israel, and David. His obedience is perfect, and he confirms the abiding goodness of God's law. Several points of application come to mind.

1. Jesus shows us what it looks like to love God and neighbor. In Jesus, perfect obedience is not antithetical to love, but he shows us the

---

[10]See Jn 7:37-38 (my translation): "If anyone thirsts, let him come to me / and let him drink, the one who believes in me. / As Scripture says, 'rivers of living water will flow from his belly.'" In this case, the living waters likely come from Jesus himself, who is presented as the final temple. See further Ezek 47:1-12; Jn 4:14; 21:1-14.

covenantal paradigm that true love is true obedience. Let it never be said, "I love God, but I don't care for his commands." The life of Jesus blows this unbiblical paradigm out of the water. In the context of God's covenant, love for God is expressed by care for and obedience to his commands.

2. Jesus not only provides us a model; he comes to save sinners. Jesus is gentle and lowly; he is rich in love and provides rest for weary souls (see Mt 11:28-30). Sin is wearisome. Life is difficult in a fallen world. Jesus knows that; he has lived in this fallen world and suffered its consequences. He knows what it's like to go without, to be without a home, and to be betrayed. Yet he is a haven of rest for those who would come to him. No normal person can earn life by obedience to God's commands; Jesus therefore grants us eternal life as a gift, freeing us from the burden of seeking to gain a standing by our own works, apart from faith. As our covenant representative, Jesus defeats the devil and delivers us from the kingdom of darkness. We don't have to win the fight against the devil; Jesus does that for us (see 1 Jn 3:8).

3. Often the life of faith is a life of waiting. Even so, while we wait we must continue to persevere by faith, walking in the light of God's law (Ps 119:105). This can be discouraging. But we must hold fast to God's covenant promises. Consider Simeon and Anna in the Gospel of Luke. Simeon was an old man, who was eagerly awaiting the consolation of Israel (Lk 2:25). Yet it had been revealed to him that he would not die before he saw the coming of the Messiah (Lk 2:26). Simeon most likely waited a long time but continued to look ahead in faith to the one God had promised. Likewise Anna was always in the temple (Lk 2:37). She was well-advanced in years, being at least eighty-four years old, and likely much older.[11] Yet Anna maintained her vigilance, devoting herself to the God of Israel.

---

[11] It's uncertain whether Lk 2:37 means that Anna was eighty-four years old, or whether she had been a widow for eighty-four years. If Anna had been a *widow* for eighty-four years, she may have been around one hundred years old.

Simeon and Anna model what it means to wait for the coming of Christ. They were waiting for the first coming of Christ. Our situation is remarkably similar today. Jesus is coming back. As we await his return, we must hold fast to God's covenant promises. The world at large is not anticipating the return of Christ. You won't find it mentioned on the evening news or in the morning newspaper. We must look to Scripture to guide us and live each day in anticipation of his return. It is easy to forget God's promises and only live by what we can see with our eyes. Temptations to assimilate to the world are strong. Yet God is in control, and in the midst of uncertain times, we can be sure that Christ will come again.

How will we live in the meantime? Will we live in Christ-conformity? Or will we instead doubt God's promises and the goodness of his law? These choices confront us daily, and we must endeavor, by the grace of God, to follow Christ today.

SUGGESTED READING

Crowe, Brandon D. *The Last Adam: A Theology of the Obedient Life of Jesus in the Gospels.* Grand Rapids, MI: Baker Academic, 2017.

Poythress, Vern S. *The Miracles of Jesus: How the Savior's Mighty Acts Serve as Signs of Redemption.* Wheaton, IL: Crossway, 2016.

Ridderbos, Herman. *The Coming of the Kingdom.* Edited by Raymond O. Zorn. Translated by H. de Jongste. Philadelphia: P&R, 1962.

Chapter Seven

THE TEACHING OF JESUS

THE LAW FULFILLED AND ABIDING

MOST PEOPLE TODAY HAVE AN OPINION ABOUT JESUS. Yet many opinions are influenced more by popular culture than by Scripture. One common trope is that Jesus is "a great moral teacher." Often this view seeks to categorize Christianity with other world religions, perhaps even suggesting that there is no qualitative difference between Jesus and most other religious teachers. However, this approach misses the uniqueness of Christ's person and work. Jesus is no ordinary man but the eternal Son of God who has taken a human nature without ceasing to be God. As the perfectly holy, righteous, and obedient last Adam, Jesus saves us from our sins and grants us eternal life. This is something no other moral teacher could ever do, since all other people are born in Adam. Jesus is sinless and divine, and thus he is qualitatively different from all other moral teachers.

The notion of Christ as divine Son of God and Savior should be uncontroversial for Christian readers. Even so, we should not jettison the notion that Jesus is a great teacher. We would miss significant aspects of the ministry of Christ if we did not have this category. But we must be more specific.

Jesus is—like Adam, David, and even Israel[1]—prophet, priest, and king. This means Jesus is not simply a moral teacher, but a *prophet* who makes known the will of God.

In the previous chapter I showed how Jesus saves us from our sins as the obedient Son of God. In this chapter we will look at Jesus' teaching about obedience in light of the salvation he accomplishes. To be sure, our relationship to the law changes when Jesus comes. For example, no longer do its ceremonial aspects govern the practice of God's people. Jesus' death puts an end to the need for ongoing sacrifices (Heb 10:14), and he himself teaches that all foods are clean (Mk 7:19). But neither has he come to abolish the law altogether (Mt 5:17). The moral aspects of God's law, seen summarily in the Ten Commandments, continue to govern the practice of God's people.[2]

In short, Jesus not only fulfills the law as the fully obedient Son of God; he also calls his people to true obedience. Jesus teaches us what the law of God truly requires: true love for God and true love for neighbor.

Most of our attention in this chapter will be given to the Sermon on the Mount (Mt 5–7) and Jesus' Farewell Discourse (Jn 13:31–16:33). In these texts Jesus teaches that true covenant blessing comes through rigorous obedience to the law of God in fellowship with Jesus himself—the one who obeys the law perfectly.

SERMON ON THE MOUNT (MATTHEW 5-7)

The Sermon on the Mount is among the most well-known portions of Scripture. Yet it is also a section that has been widely debated. Interpreters through the centuries have often given drastically different answers to the question of how (and sometimes whether!) the Sermon on the Mount applies to the church today.

---

[1]On Israel as prophet, priest, and king see Ex 19:4-6; 20–23; Benjamin L. Gladd, *From Adam and Israel to the Church: A Biblical Theology of the People of God*, ESBT (Downers Grove, IL: IVP Academic, 2019), 40-44.

[2]As noted earlier, this does not mean that the moral law of God is absolutely *limited* to the Ten Commandments, but these are the *summary* of the moral law of God. We continue to be instructed by all parts of God's law, though we do not live under the civil and ceremonial aspects of the Old Testament law in the new covenant.

Yet the Sermon on the Mount is not so different from other parts of Scripture addressing the law of God. In the Sermon on the Mount we see what God truly requires of his people: true obedience to the law of God. Obedience brings blessing, whereas rejection of God's law brings curse. In the new covenant it remains true that the life of blessing is a life of conformity to the law of God.

The Beatitudes (Mt 5:3-12). We start with the Beatitudes (Mt 5:3-12). The first one reads: "Blessed are the poor in spirit, for theirs is the kingdom of heaven" (Mt 5:3). In this opening section of the Sermon on the Mount, Jesus describes the life of blessing. It's the life described in Psalm 1—the person characterized by conformity to God's law. This is a key part of the background to the term "blessed." The blessed one who flourishes like a tree planted by streams of water is the one whose life reflects God's law and turns from wickedness.

But there's more. The term "blessed" also refers to the blessing of being redeemed by God. In fact, the last recorded words of Moses speak of the blessing of those who are redeemed by God (Deut 33:29).[3] This reminds us that the proper context for living by God's law is redemption: *God's people are redeemed in order that they might obey*. At the beginning of the Sermon of the Mount, we're reminded of redemption.[4]

The Beatitudes—and the Sermon on the Mount more broadly—cast a vision of the kingdom of heaven (e.g., Mt 5:3, 10; 6:10; 7:21). They describe the life of one who responds to the call of God in Christ and the blessings that follow. They also sketch what it looks like to follow Jesus in the kingdom, where worldly ethics are subverted and inverted. True blessing comes not from being powerful but from being meek and merciful. These are the blessings we see in Jesus himself, who shows us what it means to be meek, merciful, pure in heart, and so forth.[5]

---

[3] See Charles Quarles, *Sermon on the Mount: Restoring Christ's Message to the Modern Church*, NACSBT (Nashville: B&H Publishing, 2011), 39.

[4] Geerhardus Vos, "Hungering and Thirsting After Righteousness," in *Grace and Glory: Sermons Preached in the Chapel of Princeton Theological Seminary* (Edinburgh: Banner of Truth, 1994), 28.

[5] See Dale C. Allison Jr., "Structure, Biographical Impulse, and the *Imitatio Christi*," in *Studies in Matthew: Interpretation Past and Present* (Grand Rapids, MI: Baker Academic, 2005), 149-50.

One's relationship to Christ is crucial to understanding the Sermon on the Mount appropriately, and also to understanding our call to obedience in the new age. Law adherence must be married to Christ adherence. These are a package deal. Following Christ requires us to obey God's law, as Jesus explains in the Farewell Discourse (Jn 14:15). And obeying the law of God rightly means understanding its relationship to the one who authoritatively interprets the law and fulfills it unto salvation.

The law and greater righteousness (Mt 5:17-20). This brings us to a key text in the Sermon on the Mount. Jesus states,

> Do not think that I have come to abolish the Law or the Prophets; I have not come to abolish them but to fulfill them. For truly, I say to you, until heaven and earth pass away, not an iota, not a dot, will pass from the Law until all is accomplished. Therefore whoever relaxes one of the least of these commandments and teaches others to do the same will be called least in the kingdom of heaven, but whoever does them and teaches them will be called great in the kingdom of heaven. For I tell you, unless your righteousness exceeds that of the scribes and Pharisees, you will never enter the kingdom of heaven. (Mt 5:17-20)

This is a complicated text, but a few points are particularly important.

1. Jesus does not want us to think that he has come to do away with the law (Mt 5:17). Some portions of the Sermon on the Mount may sound like Jesus is disagreeing with or annulling the law (see Mt 5:21-48), but Jesus clarifies; that is not his purpose. The law remains relevant for God's people.

2. Jesus fulfills the law (Mt 5:17-18). Jesus is the goal of the law (Rom 10:4), and to understand the law we must understand its relationship to Jesus himself. As we saw in the previous chapter, Jesus is the perfectly obedient Son of God. The law is not understood properly in abstraction from Jesus, for the law speaks of Jesus, and only Jesus meets its rigorous demands. Jesus' fulfillment of the law should be understood in an eschatological sense. That is, Jesus has brought, by his obedience, the anticipated end-time salvation of the latter days anticipated by the Prophets. By fulfilling the law Jesus ushers in the era of fulfillment,

which is also the era of greater covenant blessing marked eventually by the outpouring of the Spirit at Pentecost (Acts 2). Yet even though Jesus fulfills the law, this does not mean that God's law passes away in this age.

3. Jesus' focus on the "least of these commandments" (Mt 5:19) highlights the importance of each command; we must not downplay the importance of God's law in the age of fulfillment. Those who downplay God's commandments and teach others to downplay God's commandments will be called "least" in the kingdom of heaven; those who keep the commandments and teach others to keep the commandments will be called "great" in the kingdom of heaven. Here the "commandments" primarily refer to the law of Moses.[6] Theologian John Murray captures this eloquently: "The criterion of our standing in the kingdom of God and of reward in the age to come is nothing else than meticulous observance of the commandments of God in the minute details of their prescription and the earnest inculcation of such observance on the part of others."[7] Stated differently, greatness in the kingdom of heaven is correlated to one's making much of the law of God.

4. Followers of Christ must exhibit a greater righteousness than the scribes and Pharisees (Mt 5:20). "Greater righteousness" does not refer to a hypothetical ideal of righteousness that no one can put into practice, as though Jesus points out the folly of trying to beat the Pharisees in their über-meticulous rule keeping. In reality, the Pharisees weren't concerned enough with the law of God. They were good at outward observance, but they missed the love and mercy that God's law really requires (Mt 7:12; 9:13; 12:7; 15:7-9; 22:28-37; 23:23; see also Is 29:13; Hos 6:6). Jesus doesn't critique the Pharisees for giving too much attention to God's law; he critiques them for not giving enough attention to God's law.[8]

---

[6]So John Murray, *Principles of Conduct: Aspects of Biblical Ethics* (Grand Rapids, MI: Eerdmans, 1957), 149-80; see also R. T. France, *The Gospel of Matthew*, NICNT (Grand Rapids, MI: Eerdmans, 2007), 184-88.

[7]Murray, *Principles of Conduct*, 154.

[8]See France, *Matthew*, 190; Craig S. Keener, *A Socio-Rhetorical Commentary on the Gospel According to Matthew* (Grand Rapids, MI: Eerdmans, 2009), 175-80; W. D. Davies and D. C. Allison Jr.,

Jesus' point is that his disciples must give careful attention to the law of God, and we must do so in relation to Jesus himself who fulfills the law of God.

You have heard it said, but I say . . . (Mt 5:21-48). Once Jesus has made it clear that he has not come to abrogate God's law, he gives six contrasting statements. In these Jesus contrasts what the people had heard with what is written in the law of God. Jesus does not disagree with the written law of God, but with misunderstandings of the law of God ("you have heard it said . . . but I say to you"). In contrast to what they may have heard, Jesus explains what the law of God really requires.

It's helpful to note that of these six statements, the first four seem to echo the Ten Commandments.[9] The Ten Commandments remain in effect but require more than we might think at first glance. The sixth commandment does not simply require us not to murder.[10] Instead, it requires us to seek reconciliation and be quick to be at peace with our neighbor (Mt 5:21-26). The seventh commandment not only prohibits the physical act of adultery but even adulterous thoughts (Mt 5:27-30). Jesus shows with particular clarity the spiritual dimensions of what God requires in his law. Yet this is not entirely new. The law was already spiritual and required true obedience in the Old Testament. Jesus does not make the law something it wasn't already but unfolds and applies it in new ways, even as he brings the law to its fulfillment as the goal to which it pointed. The law is spiritual and requires more than only outward obedience.

A summary of grace and obedience in the Sermon the Mount. The Sermon on the Mount is not an exhaustive checklist for the Christian life that gives us formulaic answers for specific scenarios. Instead, in the Sermon on the Mount Jesus provides a paradigm for life in covenant with God. The life of blessing is the life of obedience. The Sermon on the Mount casts a vision for how to love and obey God as disciples of Jesus. The Sermon assumes God's

---

A Critical and Exegetical Commentary on the Gospel According to St. Matthew, ICC, 3 vols. (Edinburgh: T&T Clark, 1988–97), 1:500.

[9]These echo the prohibitions against murder (Mt 5:21-26), adultery (Mt 5:27-32), and taking God's name in vain (Mt 5:33-37).

[10]There are various options for how to enumerate the Ten Commandments; I follow the traditional Reformed enumeration, recognizing that others number them differently.

saving actions for us in Jesus and calls us to true obedience, which has always been required of God's people.

FAREWELL DISCOURSE (JN 13:31-16:33)

Jesus also shows us what true covenantal obedience looks like in the Farewell Discourse in the Gospel of John. This passage recounts Jesus' last night with his disciples, and in these parting words he emphasizes the need for his disciples to bear the fruit of obedience. The Farewell Discourse is similar to Deuteronomy, which casts a covenantal vision for God's people to express their love for him by their obedience. Likewise, Jesus states in the Farewell Discourse that if we love him, we will do what he commands (Jn 14:15). And if we do what Jesus commands, we will be loved by his Father (Jn 14:21, 23; see also Jn 14:24). As in the old covenant, so in the new covenant: truly walking with God means walking according to his commands.

But there are new aspects in the Farewell Discourse as well. Like the Sermon on the Mount, in the Farewell Discourse obedience cannot be abstracted from one's relationship to Jesus. Jesus opens the Farewell Discourse by speaking of a new command for his disciples—that they love one another (Jn 13:34; see also Jn 15:12-13). His identification of this as a *new* command is curious since the law of Moses already requires us to love God and to love our neighbor (Deut 6:5; Lev 19:18).

In what sense is this a new command? The newness must be related to the coming of Jesus himself, who shows us clearly what this command requires in the way that he loved. Jesus points us to this conclusion: "Just as I have loved you, you also are to love one another" (Jn 13:34). This command is both old and new (1 Jn 2:7-8) because it comes from the Old Testament, and is uniquely realized by Christ himself.

This wide-ranging command to love is incumbent upon disciples of Jesus. Elsewhere Jesus summarizes the Law and Prophets as love for God and love for neighbor (e.g., Mt 22:37-40). If we love Jesus, we will love one another. Jesus also promises his Spirit to help us. The Spirit himself had been active among God's people from the beginning. But there is something new: now the Spirit is known as the Spirit who accompanied and empowered Jesus of Nazareth. The Spirit who comes to the disciples is the same Spirit who empowered Jesus for his covenantal obedience.[11] When Jesus is glorified, the Spirit—who is the Spirit of the risen Christ—will be poured out more abundantly. The Spirit of the glorified Christ brings to mind all that Jesus has done and taught us in the past,[12] so that we may participate in the now-present future age of eschatological blessing as God's obedient covenant people.

The Holy Spirit, whom Jesus says so much about in the Farewell Discourse, is also related to another central topic of the Farewell Discourse: union with Christ. The Spirit of Christ who is poured out effects union with Christ.[13] "Christ dwells in us if his Spirit dwells in us, and he dwells in us by the Spirit"[14] (see Jn 14:16-17).

Union with Christ has much to do with covenantal obedience. This is clear in the passage about the vine and the branches in Jn 15:1-11, which may be the central focus of the Farewell Discourse. Jesus tells us to abide in him in order that we might bear much fruit (Jn 15:2, 4-5). This fruit is the evidence of the life that we have in Christ. The fruit of life in Christ is the fruit of obedience and flourishing, as in Psalm 1. In fact, this fruit-bearing is the mark of a true disciple. If someone does not bear the fruit of life in Christ, they are cast off because they are not true disciples (Jn 15:6, 8). This is consistent with what we see throughout Scripture: true believers bear true fruit of righteousness and repentance. Jesus sums up the covenantal contours of law keeping well in John 15:10: "If you keep my commandments, you will abide in my love, just as I have kept my Father's commandments and abide in his love."

In the new covenant era obedience continues to be a necessary fruit of true belief. And this obedience must be tethered to Christ himself—the fully obedient one. The result of this is blessing in life—what Jesus describes as joy (Jn 15:11).

---

[11]See especially Sinclair B. Ferguson, *The Holy Spirit*, CCT (Downers Grove, IL: InterVarsity Press, 1996), 44-52; Mt 4:1; 12:22-32; Mk 1:12; 3:22-30; Lk 4:1, 14; 11:14-23; see also Acts 10:38.

[12]Jn 14:16-17, 26; 15:26-27; 16:7-15.

[13]See John Murray, *Redemption Accomplished and Applied* (Grand Rapids, MI: Eerdmans, 1955), 165-66.

[14]Murray, *Redemption*, 166.

CONCLUSION AND APPLICATION

Jesus ends the Sermon on the Mount with a comparison between a wise man who builds his house on the rock and a foolish man who builds his house on the sand (Mt 7:24-27). The house built on the rock stood firm when the winds and rains came. In contrast, the house built on the sand was devastated when pummeled by the elements. This is a familiar story, but the points Jesus makes from it may not be as widely known. Consistent with covenantal pleas throughout Scripture, Jesus states that those who build on the rock are not those who only *hear* the words of Jesus, but those who put them into *practice*. Those who build on the sand hear the words of Jesus, but they don't obey (see Jas 1:25). Obedience brings blessing; disobedience brings the curse of destruction (see Lk 11:28).

The path of those who follow Jesus must be the path of obedience to the law of God.

1. The need to obey God's moral law continues in the new covenant. The rest, freedom, and salvation that Jesus brings are not indications that we are no longer bound to obedience. Jesus never calls us to dismiss God's law, nor does he ever downplay sin. Jesus fulfills the law and also expounds the law, showing us the depths of what God requires of his people. The standards are high, and a high degree of holiness must be characteristic of God's people. The Sermon on the Mount is a sermon about the coming of the kingdom and our participation in it. To be "kingdom minded" means conformity to the rigorous paradigm set forth in the Sermon on the Mount. Kingdom people must be holy people.

   This is not contradictory to the rest that Jesus brings, for Jesus also encourages us that the life of blessing is the life of law conformity (see Mt 5:3-12). Like a train running smoothly on railroad tracks, the law of God sets forth the path of blessing. Even though we cannot obey the law of God perfectly, it continues to be the path of blessing. For it is the path of fellowship with God (see 1 Jn 1:5-8).

2. Obedience cannot be abstracted from Jesus himself. It is not possible to obey God's law rightly while rejecting Jesus, for Jesus is the goal of

the law. One of the purposes of the law is to lead us to Christ and his righteousness (see Jn 5:39-47). Honoring God means honoring Jesus, and honoring Jesus means honoring his words. The greater righteousness required in the Sermon on the Mount entails both obedience to the true requirements of the law and recognizing our need for Christ—the one who fulfills all righteousness on our behalf.

3. Jesus also clarifies and summarizes the law: the law requires us to love God and love our neighbor. This should be a delight, not a burden. As the apostle John writes: "By this we know that we love the children of God, when we love God and obey his commandments. For this is the love of God, that we keep his commandments. And his commandments are not burdensome" (1 Jn 5:2-3). Obeying God may be hard at times, but it's not burdensome. Sin is burdensome. Obedience is liberating; Christ frees us to obey.

SUGGESTED READING

Carson, D. A. *The Farewell Discourse and the Final Prayer of Jesus: An Evangelical Exposition of John 14–17*. Grand Rapids, MI: Baker, 1980.

Ferguson, Sinclair B. *The Sermon on the Mount*. Edinburgh: Banner of Truth, 1987.

Pennington, Jonathan T. *The Sermon on the Mount and Human Flourishing: A Theological Commentary*. Grand Rapids, MI: Baker Academic, 2017.

Vos, Geerhardus. *The Teaching of Jesus Concerning the Kingdom of God and the Church*. N. p. Reprint, Fontes, 2017.

Chapter Eight

THE MESSIAH AND HIS WORK EXPLAINED

ACTS AND PAUL'S LETTERS

THE WORLD IS FULL OF FASCINATING HISTORICAL SITES. Having the chance to see in person places you've read about and studied in books can be a real thrill. But it's an even more enriching experience when you're led by a seasoned guide.

If you were to show up in London having never been there before, you could certainly figure many things out on your own. You might stop at interesting places or try a local restaurant that looks good from the outside. Your experience would likely be better if you bought a travel book to guide you. The experience would be better still if you hired a famed Blue Badge tour guide. A personal and knowledgeable guide brings London to life.

In this chapter we will look at Acts and Paul's letters. Luke (the author of Luke and Acts) and Paul are knowledgeable guides who write authoritative, inspired works about Jesus. They understand the significance of Jesus, including how he relates to the Old Testament. Jesus is the king who reigns over a worldwide kingdom by means of his resurrection from the dead. He is the mediator and focal point of the new covenant community. Jesus brings the fullness of end-time blessings that the Prophets spoke of, yet sin continues to be a real danger in this age. This is the "already/not-yet" paradigm of biblical theology. We live in an in-between time, in which we *already* experience rich blessings of fulfillment, but we also face temptations and suffering since final deliverance has *not yet* come. Much of the New Testament is written to help us live practically in this interim period. Acts explains the resurrection of Jesus and how that relates to the law of God. Paul's letters work out in detail the relationship between what Jesus has done for us ("indicative") and what we are required to do as disciples ("imperative").

Acts and Paul also show us that obedience to God's law remains a requirement for his people, even if there are aspects of how we relate to the law that are different now that Christ has fulfilled the law. The grace of Christ is deeper than we can fathom, but this does not negate the need for true obedience. As we have seen throughout the Scriptures, in these books we find a familiar pattern: the life of blessing is the life of obedience to God's law. And as we saw in the previous chapter, this obedience must be obedience *in and through* Christ himself.

COVENANT AND LAW IN ACTS

Acts and covenant history. Acts begins where the Gospel of Luke ends: with the resurrected Jesus ascending to heaven. In the speeches that follow, the apostles consistently draw attention to the resurrection of Christ and its implications. Put simply, because Jesus has risen from the dead, he reigns over an everlasting kingdom (e.g., Acts 2:22-36; 13:26-37) and is the judge of all people (Acts 17:30-31). Jesus was raised from the dead because he was the fully righteous one, who was completely devoted to the will of God (Lk 23:47; Acts 2:27, 31; 3:14-15; 7:52; 13:28, 35-39; 22:14). Through his resurrection Jesus secures forgiveness of sins and justification (i.e., a right standing before God) for his people (Acts 13:38-39).

Acts also teaches that Jesus' resurrection fulfills God's covenant with David. In Luke Gabriel promised Mary that her child would reign over the kingdom of David *forever* (Lk 1:32-33). In Acts this comes to fruition, fulfilling the promise to David that he would always have a son to sit on this throne (2 Sam 7:13). David died and was buried, and his body remained in the grave (Acts 2:29; 13:36); Jesus died and was buried, and he rose from the dead (Acts 2:30-32; 13:27-30). As a prophet (Acts 2:30), David knew that the holy one who would not see corruption must be one of his offspring, who was greater than David himself (see Ps 16:10-11). David was committed to the will of God more than Saul, for David understood that obedience was better than sacrifice (Acts 13:22; see also 1 Sam 15:22). Yet despite his righteousness, David's body saw decay (Acts 13:36). The greater son of David who was buried and did not see decay must have been more fully committed to the will of God. Jesus is the *fully* righteous son of David.

Stephen also provides a survey of Israel's covenant history with particular focus on Abraham, Moses, and David (Acts 7:2-53). This speech is a response to the charge that Stephen was speaking against the temple and the law of Moses (Acts 6:13-14). Stephen explains that God is much bigger than the temple; a survey of covenant history will show many ways that God was with his people beyond the temple. No one doubted the centrality of the temple, yet God had never been *limited* to one place. Further, the temple was not permanent but pointed to Christ himself—the true temple whose glory excelled that of Solomon's temple (see Jn 1:14, 18, 51; 2:11, 20-23). Similar to the critique of Jesus in the Gospels, Stephen critiques his opponents for clinging to a particular place while disobeying the living words of God (Acts 7:38-43, 53). Covenant history is full of examples of God's covenant people rejecting the law of God; many even rejected Moses in his own day. Stephen is not rejecting the law of God. Instead, the mob who had gathered, and who would soon murder Stephen, make an idol of the temple (Acts 7:48).[1] They are just like their fathers who always resisted the Holy Spirit and disobeyed the law of God (Acts 7:51, 53).

The Prophets spoke about the coming of the Righteous One (Acts 7:52). Now that Jesus, the Righteous One, had come, it is an even more egregious sin to reject him than to reject Moses or the Prophets. Stephen's fate thus recalls the fate of Jesus himself. By embracing the coming one whom Moses and the

---

[1] The term "made with hands" is terminology for idols. Stephen uses this language to speak of the temple in Jerusalem.

Prophets foretold, Stephen is actually being more faithful to the covenant promises. Embracing Jesus does not mean rejecting the law. But it does mean recognizing that the substance to which the old covenant pointed has come.

Acts and the law in the new covenant. With the coming of Jesus in covenant history, the relationship of believers to the law changes. This is addressed at the Jerusalem Council (Acts 15). Here, early believers met to address how the church should treat the influx of Gentiles into the church. At this early stage of church history many believers in Jesus were Jewish. In accordance with the Abrahamic covenant, Jewish male children received the distinctive covenant sign of circumcision. The Jewish people also made distinctions between clean and unclean foods according to the law of Moses. Since Jesus did not reject the law (Mt 5:17-18), many thought that Gentiles had to adopt Jewish practices to participate in the new covenant community. This would mean Gentile males should be circumcised (see Acts 15:1, 5) and presumably that food laws should continue to be observed.

Yet in Acts events transpire that call this into question. Earlier Peter encountered the Gentile centurion Cornelius, who was not circumcised and yet received the outpouring of the Holy Spirit—the eschatological covenant blessing (Acts 10–11). Further, Peter's visit with Cornelius was precipitated by a threefold vision commanding Peter to eat *unclean* and therefore *unlawful* foods. Peter naturally resisted, but the message soon became clear: if God has accepted Cornelius by faith and poured out his Spirit on him, then no person is of lesser status in God's kingdom because of what he or she eats (Acts 10:28, 34-35). Peter relates these events to the Jerusalem Council. If the Holy Spirit has been poured out on the Gentiles apart from circumcision, this demonstrates that God shows no partiality among people groups (Acts 15:7-9). It therefore doesn't matter whether someone is circumcised. No one is saved by following the law of God (Acts 15:10); instead we're saved by the grace of Jesus Christ (Acts 15:11), who obeyed the law on our behalf. What matters is faith in Christ, not one's ethnic or cultural identity.

These events help those gathered at the Jerusalem Council reach their decision. Though the law is an unbearable yoke for salvation (Acts 15:10), it is not to be thrown out altogether. Distinctions must be made among aspects of God's law, especially with respect to ceremonial and moral aspects. The apostles require Gentiles to abstain from four things: from meat that has been sacrificed to idols, from blood, from things that have been strangled, and from sexual immorality (Acts 15:22-29; see also Acts 21:25). The first three items most likely deal with food and refer either to avoiding idolatrous temple feasts or avoiding certain types of food as a concession to Jewish believers (in order to promote unity in the church among those of different cultural backgrounds). If the prohibition is against idolatrous practices, then the point is clear enough—no Christian is free to participate in idolatry. But if the prohibition is against eating certain types of food for the sake of fellowship, this must be a temporary concession rather than a permanent rule. For elsewhere Peter has been shown that no person who eats unclean food is to be treated any differently (Acts 10:28, 34-35), and Paul's letters show us that it would be inconsistent with the gospel to show favoritism because of food (Gal 2:11-14; see also Rom 14:20; 1 Cor 10:25-26; 1 Tim 4:3-4).[2]

The prohibition against sexual immorality is less complicated: all sexual relations outside the parameters of biblical marriage are forbidden. This teaching on sexual purity would have been particularly important for converts from outside Judaism. Whereas the food laws are tempered when we look at other texts (e.g., Jesus declared all foods clean [Mk 7:19]), the New Testament consistently reaffirms the prohibitions against sexual immorality (e.g., 1 Thess 4:3-8).

In sum, the Jerusalem Council does not require circumcision for Gentile converts—the letter they send declaring their decision (Acts 15:23-29) does not even mention circumcision. Further, if the prohibitions regarding food are temporary concessions for the sake of unity, then the Jerusalem Council assumes distinctions between ceremonial aspects of the law that are not permanently binding and moral aspects that continue to be. Either way, the rest of the New Testament makes it clear that food laws from the Old Testament are no longer necessary. They were temporary.

The Jerusalem Council does not answer all our questions about how we obey the law now that Christ has fulfilled the law. And yet the Council does show us that the law is perpetually relevant—for all peoples—even though

---

[2]Particularly helpful here is Turretin, *Inst.* 11.25.17, 20-21 (2:163-65).

our relationship to the law is recalibrated in light of the work of Christ. Paul's epistles provide even more detail on these issues.

COVENANT AND LAW IN PAUL'S EPISTLES

The Jerusalem Council is not the final word when it comes to law and covenant in the New Testament. The apostle Paul covers the same issues—and many more besides. The following discussion will therefore be limited to covenant and law. We'll consider these in relation to three topics: the salvation accomplished by Christ, the identity of the people of God, and the obedience of the people of God.

Salvation accomplished. Paul expounds the meaning of Jesus' work as Messiah at great length, and he often does so by relating Jesus to covenant history. Jesus came as the fully faithful Israelite from the family of Abraham (Gal 3:15-20). Jesus is also the promised Son of David who brings lasting salvation (Rom 1:3-4). More fundamentally, Jesus came as the second and last Adam whose obedience overcomes the sin of Adam and rescues us from our sin (Rom 5:12-21).

Jesus and Adam. Paul views Jesus as the second and last Adam. In Romans 5:12-21 (and also in 1 Cor 15:21-28, 45-49) Paul contrasts Adam and the death that he brought into the world with Jesus and the life that he grants on account of his perfect obedience: "Therefore, as one trespass led to condemnation for all men, so one act of righteousness leads to justification and life for all men. For as by the one man's disobedience the many were made sinners, so by the one man's obedience the many will be made righteous" (Rom 5:18-19). Here the one act of righteousness, or the righteous act of one man, refers summarily to the entire obedience of Jesus. Jesus' obedience overcomes the sin of Adam and brings righteousness in place of death. As we saw earlier, Paul speaks in Romans 5 of two covenant heads of humanity: Adam and Christ.

Everyone is either "in Adam" or "in Christ." Though Adam was offered life on condition of perfect obedience, he sinned and brought death and condemnation instead (Rom 5:12). This has affected all people who come naturally from Adam. In contrast, Jesus' actions—as the last Adam and the new head of humanity—bring life to all those who are in him. Paul's discussion not only necessitates the historicity of Adam but necessitates that Adam served a representative, covenantal role and his actions have implications for those he represented. The life that Adam failed to realize because of his sin is realized by Christ, the fully obedient Son of God. For sake of reference, I include again the illustration summarizing the covenant of works and the covenant of grace (see figure 8.1).

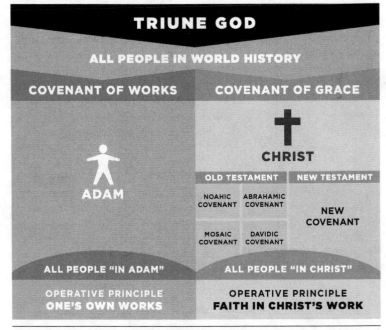

Figure 8.1. Two overarching covenants: covenant of works and covenant of grace[3]

Jesus, Abraham, and the law of Moses. Paul also speaks of the salvation accomplished by Jesus by explaining his relationship to Abraham and the law of Moses. Galatians says much about this. One of the most difficult passages in Galatians addresses the issues of law and covenant:

> For all who rely on works of the law are under a curse; for it is written, "Cursed be everyone who does not abide by all things written in the Book of the Law,

---

[3]See note to figure 1.1.

and do them." Now it is evident that no one is justified before God by the law, for "The righteous shall live by faith." But the law is not of faith, rather "The one who does them shall live by them." (Gal 3:10-12)

This text contains a number of difficult issues. For example, I argued in chapter two that the law of Moses was part of the covenant of grace and was given to God's people to provide them a guide to righteous living. The law was not given for the people of Israel to *earn* their salvation but was given to a redeemed people. But if this is the case, why does Paul state *that the law is not of faith* (Gal 3:12)? And why does he underscore the need to do *all* the things written in the Book of the Law (Gal 3:10)? It sounds like Paul is contrasting the law with faith, whereas the Old Testament called God's people to live by faith by walking according to the law.

To understand what Paul means, we need to keep two things in mind. First, there were people in Galatia who denigrated Christ by holding stubbornly to the law of Moses. They missed that the law points forward to Christ, who fulfilled the law, and who ushered in a new era of redemptive history that is not governed by the law of Moses as a covenant administration (see Rom 10:4; Gal 3:23). It is possible to "live" by the law in one respect yet miss the importance of Christ himself. If that happens, the law is of no benefit (Gal 2:19-21; 3:19, 22-24; 5:1-6).

Second, the law of Moses was given to a redeemed people, but it also attested to a principle that has been true since the days of Adam—to realize the goal of eternal life by means of law keeping requires *perfect* obedience (Gal 3:10-12; see also Lev 18:5; Deut 27:26). Paul shows the Galatians that if they attempt to be made right before God on the basis of their law keeping, then they would remain under a curse (see Gal 3:1-10). Instead, to be true children of Abraham means sharing the *faith* of Abraham. Not even Abraham was saved by his own obedience (certainly not by obedience to the law of Moses that came 430 years later), but he was declared righteous by faith alone (Gal 3:17-18; see Gen 15:6). And the promise of faith is much bigger than only one nation. The Spirit's outpouring demonstrates that all who share in the faith of Abraham—whether Jew or Gentile—share in the covenantal blessing (Gal 3:14).

The reason for this unity of Jew and Gentile is that the object of our faith has now come—Christ himself (Gal 3:23-24). Christ alone met the requirement of perfect obedience to the law of God. Christ redeemed all true believers from the curse of the law by becoming a wrath-bearing substitute on the cross (Gal 3:13). Christ became the curse that we might receive the blessing. As the substance to which the law pointed, Christ brought an end to the law as a schoolmaster (Gal 3:24-26). Jesus himself was made under the law, bearing its penalties and accomplishing its requirements, in order that we all—Jews *and* Gentiles—might receive adoption as sons of God through faith (Gal 4:1-7). We can receive the blessing because Christ has obeyed the law fully. This is why faith in Christ is necessary for justification: by being united to Christ by faith, we are treated as though we have obeyed the law perfectly. Christ not only bears our penalty, but his righteousness is legally credited to us. This all comes by faith.

Because Christ has fulfilled the law, we do not live under it as a covenant administration. But the moral law of God remains binding. Even Paul himself, who continued to live according to the law in many ways (Acts 21:24; 23:6; 1 Cor 9:20), makes it clear that he is not under the law (1 Cor 9:19-21). Yet neither is the law completely irrelevant for him, for he remains under the law of Christ (1 Cor 9:21). Those who follow Christ are not set free from the law altogether. They are still bound to obey the moral law of God. This is the law Jesus summarized as requiring love for God and love for neighbor.

Jesus and David. Jesus is also David's greater Son who brings about an everlasting kingdom by his resurrection from the dead (Rom 1:3-4). As the resurrected Lord he calls his people to the obedience of faith through the ministry of the apostles (Rom 1:5; 16:25-26). He will eventually defeat all his enemies and will even vanquish death (1 Cor 15:24-28).

The identity of God's people. One of the biggest questions facing the early church was who comprises the true people of God and how they are to be distinguished. For thousands of years circumcision had been one of the defining marks of God's people. It was therefore a tectonic shift when the apostles did not require circumcision moving forward. But circumcision is misunderstood if it is taken *only* as an external sign. The Old Testament speaks of the need for more than only physical circumcision; circumcision *of the heart* is necessary. This is another way of saying God's people needed to exhibit true faith to which circumcision pointed.

Paul addresses this issue in Romans and Galatians, and to a lesser extent Philippians and Colossians. When Christ comes circumcision is no longer necessary, because he is the goal to which circumcision points. Instead of physical circumcision, we need the circumcision of Christ (Col 2:11). This probably refers either to the circumcision Christ performs on his people, or to the circumcision experienced by Christ—that is, his death. Either way, the circumcision of Christ highlights the need to die to sin and live to God (Col 2:11-15). Physically belonging to Israel does not obviate the need for true faith in Israel's covenantal God. True children of Abraham are not those who are circumcised outwardly but those who share in the faith of Abraham (Gal 3:7-9), the man who was righteous by faith. The sign and seal of this righteousness that comes by faith is no longer circumcision but is now baptism (Rom 4:11).

In short, what matters is not circumcision, but faith in Christ. Like the Prophets, Paul critiques those who are outwardly circumcised but fail truly to love and obey God (Rom 2:25-29; 4:9-12; see also Gal 6:13; Phil 3:2-3). Paul sums it up: "For no one is a Jew who is merely one outwardly, nor is circumcision outward and physical. But a Jew is one inwardly, and circumcision is a matter of the heart, by the Spirit, not by the letter" (Rom 2:28-29). What matters is not circumcision, but faith working through love (Gal 5:6).

Paul wrestles with this issue at length: If Jesus fulfills the Old Testament, why had so many Jewish people not embraced Jesus as Messiah (see esp. Rom 9–11)? Had God turned his back on his covenant promises? Paul answers this with an emphatic "no." Paul explains that the true children of Abraham— whether they are Jews or Gentiles—share the faith of Abraham according to the promise (Rom 9:6-8; see also Rom 4:1-25). But Paul also recognizes something important from covenant history: there has always been a distinction within Israel, and true believers are often only a remnant (Rom 11:1-5). Elijah was opposed by God's covenant people and felt abandoned, but the LORD had preserved a remnant of seven thousand covenant members who had not caved to idolatry (Rom 11:3; 1 Kings 19:10, 14, 18). True covenant membership, from the very beginning, is marked not by physical birth but by faith and repentance.

On this point, it bears emphasizing that Paul writes not simply about faith in generic terms but about faith *in Christ.* Paul most often identifies Christians as those who are united to Christ by faith.[4] This has implications for our own obedience, for union with Christ does not mean being absolved from the law altogether but being under the law of Christ (Rom 6:1-14; 1 Cor 9:21). As Sinclair Ferguson comments, "the new-covenant believer never looks at the law without understanding that his relationship to it is the fruit of his union with Christ."[5]

Further, faith in Christ bears the fruit of obedience, as it did for Abraham.[6] Justifying faith is an active, obedience-working faith. Abraham's true children follow his pattern of righteousness by faith. Paul makes it abundantly clear that the moral aspects of the law continue to be binding. Thankfully, Paul devotes a significant amount of space in his letters to explaining the sort of obedience that is required for true covenant members today, who live after the coming of Christ in history.

The obedience of God's people. God's new covenant people are still bound to obey the law of God. On the one hand, observing circumcision, food laws, and holy days is not necessary.[7] On the other hand, Paul reconfirms the moral law of God, summarized in the Ten Commandments. Christ as the end or goal of the law (Rom 10:4) does not negate our ongoing need to obey the law *in light of Christ.* Christ brings an end to the law as a schoolmaster but not to the moral law as a guide for life.

Galatians again illustrates this. After vigorously arguing that adherence to the law of Moses is not required for those who follow Christ, Paul explains that obedience to the law of God remains necessary! This could be confusing, but Paul helps us quite a bit. He tells us that we are called to freedom in Christ (Gal 5:1). Yet this is not a freedom to sin, for that would be bondage

---

[4]See, e.g., Rom 5:18–6:14; 16:7; 1 Cor 1:2, 5, 30; 6:17; 15:22; 2 Cor 5:17; Gal 2:16, 20; Eph 1:1-14; 2:7, 13; 3:12; Phil 2:1; Col 1:2; 3:1, 3.

[5]Sinclair B. Ferguson, *The Whole Christ: Legalism, Antinomianism, and Gospel Assurance—Why the Marrow Controversy Still Matters* (Wheaton, IL: Crossway, 2016), 160. See also Rom 14:20; 1 Cor 8–10; Col 2:16-17; 1 Tim 4:3.

[6]See, e.g., Mt 3:8-9; Lk 3:8-9; Jn 8:39-40; Heb 11:8; Jas 2:21-23; see also Rom 4:10-12.

[7]E.g., Rom 14:20; 1 Cor 8–10; Col 2:16-17; 1 Tim 4:3. Circumcision was commanded of Abraham but was also codified in the law of Moses (Lev 12:3).

(Gal 5:13). Instead, we should love one another and thus fulfill the intent of the law (Gal 5:13-14; 6:2). Since the covenant blessing of the Spirit has been poured out on the Gentiles as well as Jews, all should walk by the Spirit (Gal 5:16-18). Even though we are not *under* the law, walking by the Spirit means putting to death deeds of the flesh, including sexual immorality, idolatry, sorcery, strife, envy, and drunkenness (Gal 5:19-21). Many of these echo the Ten Commandments, such as idolatry (first and second commandment), sorcery (third commandment), sexual immorality (seventh commandment), outbursts of anger (sixth commandment; see also Mt 5:21-22), and envy (tenth commandment).[8]

Instead of indulging in fleshly behavior, Paul provides perspective on what it means to obey the law. Obeying the law means more than only *avoiding* sinful desires; following the lead of Jesus, obeying God means positively doing good: love, joy, peace, patience, kindness, goodness, faithfulness (Gal 5:22-23; see also Mt 5:21-48). Elsewhere Paul explains that the eighth commandment requires more than only not stealing; it requires us to work hard for the benefit of our neighbor (Eph 4:28). It's not enough simply to avoid inappropriate chatter; instead, we must use our words positively for the building up of the body of Christ (Eph 4:29). This is what it means to love one another and so fulfill the law. Paul sums this up in Romans:

> Owe no one anything, except to love each other, for the one who loves another has fulfilled the law. For the commandments, "You shall not commit adultery, You shall not murder, You shall not steal, You shall not covet," and any other commandment, are summed up in this word: "You shall love your neighbor as yourself." Love does no wrong to a neighbor; therefore love is the fulfilling of the law. (Rom 13:8-10; see also Gal 5:14)

Paul's frequent calls to obedience are not given for people to earn their salvation, but they are particularly directed to those who have been granted new life in Christ. New life in Christ does not mean disregarding the moral law of God but reflecting the obedience of the Savior whose obedience secures our salvation. This again reflects the indicative-imperative structure of law

---

[8]Paul also identifies covetousness as idolatry in Col 3:5.

and covenant. The "indicative" refers to how God acts to save us apart from our works. The "imperative" refers to how we must live as disciples. As we have seen throughout this study, true covenant membership requires true obedience. Yet our obedience is only possible because of the redemption God enacts on our behalf (compare, e.g., Deut 6:20-25).

This indicative-imperative relationship clarifies the connection Paul frequently makes between the new life we have been freely granted in Christ and the requirement of obedience. In Romans 6, Paul discusses union with Christ. If we have been united to Christ in his death, then just as Christ was raised to new life, so we also have been raised to walk in new obedience (Rom 6:3-4). Once we were enslaved to sin, but now we have died to sin and are no longer enslaved to it. Why would we then walk in sin, putting ourselves under its burdensome yoke willingly? We must understand that we are dead to sin, and we must not allow ourselves to be enslaved to sin. Instead, we must now live to righteousness and we must live obediently unto God, which befits those who are under grace (Rom 6:5-14).

This means that if we are in Christ, our old self has been crucified, and we are now enabled to walk in true obedience by the Spirit. It is therefore incumbent upon us to put to death our old self and walk according to our new selves, in righteousness and holiness (Eph 4:20-24; see also Col 3:5-17). Putting off the old self means putting off sinful actions that run contrary to the law of God, and instead walking in love (Eph 5:2). God has chosen us in Christ that we would be holy before him, which refers both to our status before God and to our manner of life (Eph 1:1, 4).[9]

We live now in the age of fulfillment, which entails a greater glory (2 Cor 3:5-18) and should lead to greater obedience, for now the Spirit has been poured out abundantly. The law remains good (Rom 7:12, 16), but it was always powerless to save (Rom 7:24-25). The ministry of Moses exhibited a true but limited glory. Now that the Lord Jesus has come and fulfilled the law, there is greater freedom (2 Cor 3:17), and we are being transformed after the image of Christ. By fulfilling the demands of the law perfectly, Jesus sets us free from the burden of perfect obedience.

---

[9]See Andrew T. Lincoln, *Ephesians*, WBC 42 (Nashville: Thomas Nelson, 1990), 24.

Even so, the freedom that Christ brings from sin and the law is a struggle in this age. We therefore must walk by the Spirit. This is Paul's point in Galatians 5:16-18 and perhaps in Romans 7:14-25. In Romans 7 Paul portrays a struggle in which "I" desire the good but do evil (Rom 7:19). This passage has a long tradition of being interpreted as the Christian's ongoing struggle against sin. Yet many recently have made strong arguments that the "I" Paul speaks of is not himself but the experience of someone else—perhaps Israel under the old covenant.[10] Even so, the traditional interpretation of Romans 7, which focuses on the already/not-yet struggle of the Christian, need not be abandoned. Paul's struggle against sin seems to be something that is particularly fitting for a Christian, who has inherited from Adam a mortal body that can be described as fleshly (*sarkinos*, Rom 7:14; see also Rom 13:14).[11]

Whichever interpretation you prefer for Romans 7, Christ is the answer to Paul's exasperation (Rom 7:24-25): Who shall deliver us from the body of death? Thanks be to God that in Jesus Christ we are free from the condemnation of the law, and free to fulfill the righteous requirement of the law as we walk by the Spirit (Rom 8:4). Indeed, Romans 8:4 "is conclusive proof that the law of God has the fullest normative relevance in that state which is the product of grace."[12] In Christ we are free to obey the law.

---

[10]On this view, it would be strange for Paul to speak of his own Christian experience in terms of a fleshly person sold under sin (Rom 7:14), captive to the law (Rom 7:23), and a wretched man in need of deliverance (Rom 7:24). For elsewhere Paul speaks of freedom from the law and sin (see Rom 6:1-23). It would be more consistent with what Paul says elsewhere to view the struggle of Romans 7 as someone who is not empowered by God's Spirit. See G. K. Beale, *A New Testament Biblical Theology: The Unfolding of the Old Testament in the New* (Grand Rapids, MI: Baker Academic, 2011), 844-47; Dennis E. Johnson, "The Function of Romans 7:13-25 in Paul's Argument for the Law's Impotence and the Spirit's Power, and Its Bearing on the Schizophrenic 'I,'" in *Resurrection and Eschatology: Theology in the Service of the Church. Essays in Honor of Richard B. Gaffin, Jr.*, ed. Lane G. Tipton and Jeffrey C. Waddington (Phillipsburg, NJ: P&R, 2008), 3-59; Colin G. Kruse, *Paul's Letter to the Romans*, PNTC (Grand Rapids, MI: Eerdmans, 2012), 305.

[11]See Will N. Timmins, *Romans 7 and Christian Identity: A Study of the 'I' in its Literary Context*, SNTSMS 170 (Cambridge: Cambridge University Press, 2017), 139-47; Thomas R. Schreiner, *Romans*, BECNT, 2nd ed. (Grand Rapids, MI: Baker Academic, 2018), 383-91; see also Sinclair B. Ferguson, *The Holy Spirit*, CCT (Downers Grove, IL: InterVarsity Press, 1996), 153-62.

[12]John Murray, *The Epistle to the Romans*, 2 vols., NICNT (Grand Rapids, MI: Eerdmans, 1959–65), 1:283; see also Beale, *New Testament Biblical Theology*, 878-79.

In some ways, then, Paul continues to uphold the validity of the law. For example, Paul urges obedience to the Ten Commandments and speaks of the reward for keeping them—he identifies the commandment to honor one's father and mother as the first commandment with a promise, motivating children to obey their parents (Eph 6:1-3; see also Col 3:20). It's also instructive that Paul addresses both parents *and children* in the Lord, reflecting the familial-covenantal context found throughout Scripture.[13] In the New Testament God continues to work through families.[14] Addressing children directly demonstrates that Paul assumes the children of believers are part of God's covenant community.[15]

While Paul sees rewards for keeping the commandments, he also warns against a misrepresentation of God's grace that downplays the necessity of obedience. With all that Paul says about the lavish grace of God in Christ, perhaps it can be easy to overlook Paul's strong warnings against sin. But covenantal warnings are also prevalent in his letters. Paul anticipates objections to God's grace in Christ, especially the objection that if we are saved by grace alone, then our actions do not matter (e.g., Rom 6:1, 15; Gal 2:17). But Paul vigorously objects to this notion. He warns the churches against persisting in sin and urges them not to be deceived. No one who persists in unrighteous living will inherit the kingdom of God (1 Cor 6:9; Gal 5:21; see also Rom 1:18-32). This is not a hypothetical warning that has no teeth for God's people but a bedrock principle that is not negated in the name of grace; true believers must shun sinful lifestyles.

These warnings illustrate the new covenantal context from which Paul operates: as in the old covenant, so in the new—not all those in the covenant community are true covenant members (see 1 Cor 5:9-13). Paul urges the churches not to be deceived into thinking that sin is no big deal; it is because

---

[13]That Paul addresses slaves and masters in the following verses does not discredit this abiding covenantal context, for the husband/wife and parent/child relationships are rooted in creation, whereas the master/slave relationship is not. See further S. M. Baugh, *Ephesians*, EEC (Bellingham, WA: Lexham Press, 2016), 512.

[14]I'm particularly indebted to Sinclair Ferguson for this point.

[15]See the discussion of Baugh, *Ephesians*, 503-9; see also Robert Letham, *A Christian's Pocket Guide to Baptism* (Fearn, Ross-Shire: Christian Focus, 2012), 94-101; John Murray, *Christian Baptism* (Phillipsburg, NJ: P&R, 1980), 63-64.

of sinfulness that the wrath of God comes against humanity (Eph 5:6; Col 3:6; see also Rom 1:18; Gal 6:7-8). Paul speaks of many sorts of sinfulness, but there is a notable emphasis in his letters (as in the Jerusalem Council) on the dangers of sexual immorality (Rom 1:24-27; 1 Cor 5:1-2, 11; 6:9–7:40; 2 Cor 12:21; Gal 5:19-21; Eph 4:17-19; 5:3-6; Col 3:5-8; 1 Thess 4:3-8; 1 Tim 1:8-11).

In sum, Paul teaches the churches that with the coming of Christ comes an end to the Mosaic law as a covenant administration. The law anticipated the coming of Christ. Yet Christ does not release us from the moral law of God. True experience of God's grace leads not to unholiness but to an increasing likeness of our Savior. Paul continues the covenantal perspective on the law we have seen throughout Scripture: true love for God manifests itself in true obedience. We must not participate only outwardly in God's covenant community, but we must be sure that outward rites are married to a circumcised heart. Again the pattern remains: blessings for obedience, curses for disobedience. Yet ultimately the blessing comes through Christ, who became a curse for us.

This is part of the good news of the gospel. After providing his fullest exposition of the salvation accomplished by Christ, Paul encourages his readers in their obedience and urges us all to be wise with respect to what is good and blameless with respect to what is evil (Rom 16:19). He then reminds us that the God of peace will soon crush Satan under our feet (Rom 16:20). Victory is secure through Jesus Christ.

CONCLUSION AND APPLICATION

In Acts and the Pauline epistles we are led by trustworthy and authoritative guides who help us understand what has changed now that Christ has come, and what does not change. I mention here a few points of application:

1. There is nothing that sinners can do to earn eternal life. Eternal life is given as a gift, on the basis of Jesus' representative work on our behalf. Salvation is by grace alone through faith alone, apart from our works (Eph 2:8-9). Additionally, since the fall of Adam, this has always been the true way to salvation. Abraham and David were saved by faith no less than Peter or John.

2. Though we cannot earn salvation by our obedience, those who believe in Jesus are required to walk according to the commands of God (Eph 2:10). Grace in the present age does not negate the law any more than grace in the old covenant era negated the need for law. In fact, the New Testament writers often point to selfish indulgence in the name of grace as a gross and dangerous misunderstanding of the gospel.[16]

3. As we consider how to walk according to God's commands in this age, sexual immorality is a particularly dangerous snare. The sexual ethics of God's people should be different from the world's. From the beginning, the Bible sets forth the pattern of marriage between one man and one woman for life (see Mt 19:3-9). Sexual relations outside of marriage are consistently and uniformly prohibited. Sexual immorality is defined at length in the law of God, which must inform how we define sexual immorality today.[17] This does not significantly change from the Old Testament to the New Testament. The New Testament confirms and extends the Old Testament's teaching on the need for sexual purity.[18]

A stark example in this regard is the Corinthians. Paul rebukes the Corinthians for their sexual looseness and explains that sexual immorality was antithetical to life in Christ. Those who are characterized by sexual immorality will not inherit the kingdom of God (1 Cor 5:1-2; 6:9-10; see also Heb 13:4), and such sinful activity must be dealt with in the church (1 Cor 5:2, 9-13; see also 2 Cor 12:21). There is most assuredly forgiveness for sexual sin for those who repent and turn to Christ, but to embrace as good what God has said otherwise leads to destruction.

Thus marriage and the marriage bed must be honored (Heb 13:4). Further, marriage is one of the preeminent ways that the mystery of Christ and the church is set forth (Eph 5:22-33). Sexual relations should

---

[16]E.g., Rom 6:1, 12-14; Eph 5:3-6; 2 Pet 2:2; Jude 4; see also 1 Cor 6:9-11; 2 Pet 3:16.
[17]E.g., Ex 20:14; Deut 5:18; Lev 18.
[18]Some examples include Acts 15:20; Rom 1:24-27; 1 Cor 6:9-11; Eph 4:19-20; 5:3-6; Col 3:5-6; 1 Thess 4:3-8; 1 Pet 4:3; 2 Pet 2:1-22; Jude 4, 7-8.

be held in esteem in the context of marriage, yet only in such a context. One early Christian writer captured the distinctiveness of Christianity memorably: "They share their food but not their wives."[19]

God's people must flee from all forms of sexual immorality, even if this seems strange to the world (see 1 Pet 4:4).

4. Despite the opposition of this age, we can be assured that Jesus reigns in heaven as the living, exalted king. He reigns over an everlasting kingdom and will return to restore all things (see Acts 3:21). By his resurrection, Jesus has restored the Davidic dynasty (Acts 15:16-17; see also Acts 2:30-36), defeating sin and enabling justification (Acts 13:38-39). He is the one king who unites all of God's people and pours out the blessing of the Spirit. He is also the priest who serves on our behalf in the heavenly sanctuary. And he is the prophet who has been raised up and to whom we must listen (Acts 3:22-23), for he definitively declares to us the will of God. Yet he also definitively fulfilled the will of God, freeing us from the burden of seeking life on the basis of our own obedience. Instead, we walk by faith in the final Prophet, Priest, and King—the one who sums up and surpasses the key institutions of the Old Testament.

SUGGESTED READING

Gaffin, Richard B., Jr. *By Faith, Not by Sight: Paul and the Order of Salvation*. Waynesboro, GA: Paternoster, 2006.

Green, Bradley G. *Covenant and Commandment: Works, Obedience, and Faithfulness in the Christian Life*. NSBT 33. Downers Grove, IL: InterVarsity Press, 2014.

Murray, John. *Principles of Conduct: Aspects of Biblical Ethics*. Grand Rapids, MI: Eerdmans, 1957.

_____. *Redemption Accomplished and Applied*. Grand Rapids, MI: Eerdmans, 1955.

---

[19]*Diognetus* 5:7. Translation is from Michael W. Holmes, ed., *The Apostolic Fathers: Greek Texts and English Translations*, 3rd ed. (Grand Rapids, MI: Baker Academic, 2007), 703.

Chapter Nine

THE NEW COVENANT
IN PRACTICE

HEBREWS THROUGH JUDE

"NEW" MEANS DIFFERENT THINGS TO DIFFERENT PEOPLE.
For some, buying a new car may mean a car that has just recently come off
the production line. For others, purchasing a new car means acquiring a car
with several thousand miles on it. It all depends on what we mean by "new."

The same is true for the new covenant. The Bible is clear that the new
covenant is new; but questions remain about *how* new it is. Is it absolutely
new? This can't be, since the new covenant fulfills the anticipations of
what has come before. Those in the history of the church who have argued
that the teaching of the New Testament is fundamentally at odds with
the Old Testament have rightly been deemed heretical.[1] At the same time,
the new covenant is not simply a continuation of what has come before.
It is new.

---

[1] The most famous example is Marcion of Sinope, the second-century heretic who was roundly
condemned by orthodox Christian leaders.

Hashing out the newness of the new covenant is a difficult task, and it's no surprise that Christian traditions do this in slightly different ways. Yet some things do not change. The God of the New Testament is the same God of the Old Testament. The New Testament's teaching of salvation by grace through faith is not a new way of salvation but continues the path of salvation by grace through faith from the Old Testament. Likewise, the call to obey God's law, which has been necessary from the beginning, continues to bind all people—especially Christians—in the new era marked by the outpouring of the Holy Spirit.

In what follows I will seek to explain some of the ways that new covenant is new, and some ways that it continues what has come before. Particularly helpful in this regard is the book of Hebrews, which often uses old covenant examples to encourage faithfulness in the new covenant era. The author of Hebrews warns God's people not to abandon the covenant. I will also consider the teaching of James through Jude, also known as the Catholic (or General) Epistles. These seven letters plead with God's people to cling to the true, apostolic teaching and persevere in obedience, for the atrophic tendency toward worldly assimilation is relentless.

COVENANT AND LAW IN HEBREWS

The letter of Hebrews has much to say about the new covenant, and about what is required of God's people in the new covenant era. The new covenant is mediated by Jesus Christ (Heb 8:6; 9:15; 12:24). He is the great high priest who serves in the heavenly sanctuary in the presence of God (Heb 1:3; 4:14; 6:19-20; 8:1-2; 9:24). He is also better than any earthly priest, for he is able both to understand and to help us in our weaknesses (Heb 4:15; 5:2). He shares in our flesh and blood, and has even experienced death, overcoming it through his resurrection (Heb 2:5-18). Yet this mediator is not only a true man, but also the eternal Son of God, who is the final, ultimate revelation of God (Heb 1:1-3).

What the blood of bulls and goats could never do—truly take away sin— Jesus has done by the once offering up of himself as a sacrifice for sin (Heb 10:1-4, 10-14). As the great high priest Jesus is also unique because he offers *himself* as the final covenant sacrifice (Heb 7:27; 9:24-28). The dichotomy between sacrifice and obedience had long been a problem among God's covenant people. How often had the people offered a sacrifice while their hearts were far from God? Yet this problem is overcome in the bodily offering of Jesus Christ himself.[2] For Jesus delighted to do the will of God at all times; never did he stray from the law's requirements (Ps 40:6-8; Heb 10:5-9). What God required was not mere offering but true obedience. This requirement is realized in Jesus Christ, our great high priest who gave himself as the final sacrifice, superior to any old covenant sacrifice.

Yet despite the newness and "betterness" of the new covenant (Heb 7:22; 8:6), Hebrews also speaks of covenant continuity. There is not an *absolute* antithesis between the old covenant and the new covenant; instead, it is a *relative* newness. The sacrificial system was sufficient for the old era, but *in comparison to* and *in light of* the new covenant, the old covenant is insufficient and ineffectual. Even so, the author of Hebrews has much to say about *continuity* between the old covenant and the new covenant. For example, when the author warns the people not to fall away from the living God, he appeals to the negative example of Israel's wilderness warnings (Ps 95:7-11; Heb 3:7-11). Perhaps we read the Old Testament and are bewildered at how stiff-necked the people were to reject God after all the miraculous deeds he had done for them. Surely, we think, we are in a different situation from them and would never do such a thing.

The author of Hebrews warns us otherwise. He did not view the Israelites' experience as essentially different from Christians in the new covenant era. In fact, he uses their experience as a warning for us today, noting that the gospel was preached to them (in the Old Testament!) just as it has been in the new covenant era (Heb 4:2, 6). Moreover, their status as a wandering, pilgrim people illustrates well the church's current situation as a pilgrim people in the midst of an unbelieving world.[3]

This helps us understand one of the most discussed aspects of the theology of Hebrews: the warning passages (Heb 2:1-4; 3:7–4:13; 5:11–6:12; 10:19-39; 12:1-29). Perhaps the most discussed warning passage is Hebrews 6:4-6:

---

[2]See William L. Lane, *Hebrews 1–8*, WBC 47A (Nashville: Thomas Nelson, 1991), cxxxiv; Lane, *Hebrews 9–13*, WBC 47B (Nashville: Thomas Nelson, 2000), 266.

[3]E.g., Heb 4:1-13; 11:1-40; 13:14.

> For it is impossible, in the case of those who have once been enlightened, who have tasted the heavenly gift, and have shared in the Holy Spirit, and have tasted the goodness of the word of God and the powers of the age to come, and then have fallen away, to restore them again to repentance, since they are crucifying once again the Son of God to their own harm and holding him up to contempt. (Heb 6:4-6)

Some have argued that the warning passages, such as this one, teach that someone can lose his or her salvation. For example, being enlightened and sharing in the Holy Spirit sounds like the experience of true Christians. This passage, however, does *not* teach that true salvation can be lost. On the other hand, others have suggested that the warnings are only *hypothetical* and do not reflect the possibility that one can lose his or her salvation. Both of these approaches are insufficient.

A better approach perceives a close relationship between God's old covenant people and his new covenant people. Psalm 95, which is quoted in Hebrews 3–4, is a warning against the unbelief of the wilderness generation. Yet the wilderness generation had the gospel preached to them, just as it is also preached in the new covenant era (Heb 4:2). This must mean that the spiritual situation of God's people in the new covenant era is not essentially different from the spiritual situation of God's people in the old covenant era. The old covenant community was a mixed community, comprising both true believers and those who were a part of the community but did not truly believe. God's people collectively therefore had to be warned and exhorted to obey; the tendency to turn their backs on God was a clear and present danger—even for those in the corporate covenant community.

Yet this covenant community, which includes true believers and those who did not truly believe, was blessed collectively with the words of God and even experienced powerful demonstrations of the Spirit among them. At the same time, they had to be warned to love God truly and not rely on external religious rites, lest the covenant curses fall upon them. The warning passages echo the Old Testament, illustrating the continuity between the old and new covenant communities. In both cases, the covenant community is a *mixed* community—it includes both true believers and unbelievers. The danger of unbelief within the community persists (see Heb 3:19). Though Jesus eradicated the dichotomy between obedience and sacrifice, that dichotomy persists in the covenant community in this age. In other words, *the warning passages in Hebrews are covenantal warnings for God's covenant people.*

As we see so often in the New Testament, Hebrews speaks of the new covenant as an "already and not-yet" reality. The new covenant has truly come, but it has not yet come fully. This is evident in the continued warnings for God's covenant people, including the use of an important new covenant text: Jeremiah 31:31-34. This passage is quoted at length in Hebrews 8:8-12. It is striking that the author's use of Jeremiah 31 in Hebrews 10:15-17 propels him into another *warning* (Heb 10:19-39). If we have been set apart by the blood of the covenant, how will we stand if we then trample that blood underfoot by rejecting the one sacrifice that is able to take away our sins (Heb 10:26-29)? This makes best sense if the author works within a covenantal framework in which God's people collectively are holy and set apart in one sense, though this does not guarantee that all in the covenant community truly believe. This is why God will judge his people (Heb 10:30; see also Deut 32:36).

As in the old covenant, so in the new: faithlessness among God's covenant people is a problem that must be addressed. Yet the new covenant is indeed a better and unbreakable covenant, grounded on the finished work of Christ. Its promises are certain for all who truly trust in Christ (i.e., *true* covenant members), though in this sinful age the covenant community continues to be a mixture of wheat and chaff. When Christ returns and the new covenant is consummated, then all of God's people will truly know him, and Jeremiah's vision of the new covenant will be fully realized. But we live in the mixed era of the already *and* not yet.

In spite of the persistent reality of sin, Hebrews also offers us good news. The answer to the warning passages is not in ourselves—for indeed, we are warned against the hardness of our own hearts (Heb 3:12-13). The answer instead comes from outside of us, from our merciful and faithful high priest, who intercedes for us in the inner, heavenly sanctuary, where our hope resides (Heb 6:19; see also Heb 4:14-16; 9:24).[4]

---

[4]Compare Lane, *Hebrews 1–8*, 153-54.

How then should we live? Not according to the cultic law; Hebrews is emphatic that Christ has done away with sacrifices, and to turn back to the sacrificial system would be to turn our backs on Christ (Heb 10:4, 26-31). Nor according to the civil law, for Israel is no longer a theocracy. Instead, we live according to the law written on our hearts (see Jer 31:33; Heb 8:10; 10:16). Sinclair Ferguson captures it well:

> *Which laws* are written into our minds and on our hearts? The most obvious answer is: What other law would the first readers understand but the Decalogue? Since the author of Hebrews teaches that the ceremonial patterns of the old covenant have been fulfilled in Christ, he could not have meant them. And since Hebrews was written to those who now have "no lasting city" and therefore no longer see themselves as citizens of a state with its capital in Jerusalem [Heb. 13:14], they are no longer a people governed by the civil regulations intended for life in the land.[5]

Hebrews shows us that in the new covenant the dichotomy between internal and external religion would be overcome, because the law would be written not on stone, but on the hearts of God's people. This is a new work of God in the new covenant. At the same time, the law was already written on the hearts of the truly regenerate in the old covenant (Deut 10:16; Ps 40:8).[6] What then is new? To answer this we must appreciate the coming of Christ himself, who delighted to do his Father's will, was perfectly obedient, and fulfilled the law's demands.[7] Christ inaugurated the unbreakable new covenant, and is himself the one, heavenly Mediator, rendering earthly mediators unnecessary.[8] And through Christ, the internal work of God is clearer, richer, fuller, and more extensive.

---

[5]Sinclair B. Ferguson, *The Whole Christ: Legalism, Antinomianism, and Gospel Assurance—Why the Marrow Controversy Still Matters* (Wheaton, IL: Crossway, 2016), 145 (emphasis original).

[6]E.g., Irenaeus, *Against Heresies* 4.16.3; Turretin, *Inst.* 12.2.29 (2:184); G. K. Beale, *A New Testament Biblical Theology: The Unfolding of the Old Testament in the New* (Grand Rapids, MI: Baker Academic, 2011), 732.

[7]Here I am following Brandon D. Crowe, "The Passive *and* Active Obedience of Christ: Retrieving a Biblical Distinction," in *The Doctrine on which the Church Stands or Falls: Justification in Biblical, Theological, Historical, and Pastoral Perspective*, ed. Matthew Barrett (Wheaton, IL: Crossway, 2019), 463. Further documentation can be found there.

[8]See Beale, *New Testament Biblical Theology*, 731-40. I am also indebted to Sinclair Ferguson for this emphasis on mediation.

Additionally, Christ not only saves us by his final, perfect sacrifice but also shows us that obedience to God that should be our delight as well. In the new covenant era—the era of salvation accomplished—the greater outpouring of the Holy Spirit and the freer access we have to God (Heb 4:14-16) lead to the possibility of greater obedience, even while the dangers of falling away remain acute.

COVENANT AND LAW IN THE CATHOLIC EPISTLES (JAMES THROUGH JUDE)

The Catholic or General Epistles (James through Jude) also add to our understanding of what is required of God's people in this age. These letters are quite relevant for us today since many of them were written closer to the end of the apostolic era, and they wrestle with how to live in an ungodly world in the absence of the apostles. If Christ has come and fulfilled the law, but we continue to wait for his return, how should we live in the interim?

The answer, in short, is we should continue to walk by faith and cling to the commandments. The epistle of James, for example, is concerned that Christians follow the commandments and love one another (Jas 2:8). Like the Prophets and Jesus, he warns against being mere hearers of the law and not doers of the law (Jas 1:22-24). Religious practices that are merely external are insufficient. Instead, true religious devotion is seen caring for the downtrodden and in keeping ourselves unstained from the world (Jas 1:26-27). James says nothing explicitly about Christians obeying the ceremonial aspects of the law, but he is quite concerned that we obey the moral law of God.[9] We are commanded to keep the law of liberty (Jas 1:25; 2:12)—that is, the law understood in relation to Jesus and his message.[10] We don't pick and choose which laws to follow, but we are bound to the entire moral law of God (Jas 2:10-12). James also confirms that obedience leads to blessing (Jas 1:25). It is countercultural to think that blessing and liberty come from obedience to God's law, but this is what the entire Bible teaches (see 2 Pet 2:19).

---

[9]See similarly Richard Bauckham, *James*, NTR (London: Routledge, 1999), 147. See, e.g., Jas 5:12, echoing the third commandment and Jesus' teaching in Mt 5:33-37.

[10]See Douglas J. Moo, *The Letter of James*, PNTC (Grand Rapids, MI: Eerdmans, 2000), 94; Dan G. McCartney, *James*, BECNT (Grand Rapids, MI: Baker Academic, 2009), 123-24.

The audience of 1 Peter, likely comprising mainly Gentiles, is identified as God's elect, covenant people (1 Pet 1:1). They are sprinkled with the blood of Jesus (1 Pet 1:2), which echoes Israel's covenantal sprinkling at Mount Sinai (Ex 24:8). Later Peter speaks of his readers as those who were not a people but who are now God's people. They are a royal priesthood and a holy nation (1 Pet 2:9-10; see also 1 Pet 1:12), again echoing events at Mount Sinai and God's declaration of Israel as his special people (Ex 19:5-6). Exodus 19 states that Israel will be God's treasured possession if they obey the LORD and keep his covenant; Peter's message reiterates this covenantal paradigm in several ways. He addresses his audience as exiles and strangers in this world, who must resist the spirit of this age and be holy unto the Lord (1 Pet 1:1; 2:11). They are identified as "obedient children" (1 Pet 1:14), which echoes the covenantal privilege and responsibility of Israel in the Pentateuch (and the Prophets). Israel was God's son (Ex 4:22-23; Deut 1:31; 8:5; 14:1; 32:4-6, 18-20, 43); therefore, their obedience was required (Deut 8:6; 14:1-2; see also Deut 32:4-6, 20). Peter calls his readers to be holy, for their God is holy (1 Pet 1:15-16). Here Peter quotes from Leviticus (Lev 11:44-45; 19:2), reminding us that there are perpetually abiding aspects of the law of God beyond only the Ten Commandments.

Peter explains several ways to be holy as sojourners in this world. He tells us to abstain from passions of the flesh (1 Pet 2:11), to obey earthly rulers (1 Pet 2:13-17), to love and serve our fellow Christians (1 Pet 2:17; 4:8-11), how to live with one another in households (1 Pet 2:18–3:7), and to abstain from sexual immorality with sobriety (1 Pet 4:3-4). All this we do, recognizing that the end of all things is near (1 Pet 4:7). Though the way of obedience is the way of blessing, Peter also warns us that we will face opposition in this world for following Christ (1 Pet 2:12, 15, 19-20; 3:9-17; 4:1-2, 4-5, 16). If Christ who did nothing wrong was mistreated (1 Pet 2:21-25; 3:18), we ought not to be surprised when our holiness in this world leads to persecution (1 Pet 4:12-13). And if we share in Christ's sufferings, we will in fact be blessed (1 Pet 4:14-15; see also 1 Pet 4:19).

Like Hebrews, the Catholic Epistles also warn us about dangers even *within* the covenant community. As in the old covenant, so in the new: the covenant community includes both true believers and those who reject the God of the covenant. One way we see this is in Peter's warnings against false teachers—they claim that the Lord has bought them, but they deny him by their teachings and their actions (2 Pet 2:1). They are lustful and greedy, and they downplay the return of Christ (2 Pet 2:2-3, 9-20; 3:3-4, 8-10). Peter even says it would have been better for them not to have known the word of truth than for them to have received it and turned their back on it (2 Pet 2:20-22). This refers to those *inside* the church who prey on the weak (2 Pet 2:14, 18). Similarly, Jude speaks of those who sneak in and pervert the gospel by promoting sensuality (Jude 4; see also Jude 7-8).

Similar to the Gospel of John, the letters of John also reveal a covenantal context in which obeying God demonstrates one's love for God (1 Jn 2:3-6; 3:22-23; 5:2-3; 2 Jn 6). True fellowship with God, as we see in passages like Leviticus 26, means walking in obedience to his commands (1 Jn 1:5-7). Not all those who are or who have been part of the covenant community are true covenant members (1 Jn 2:19); true covenant members believe in Jesus and walk in his ways (1 Jn 2:6; 3:23; 5:2-3). True love for God means walking in the light of God's word and not loving the world (1 Jn 2:15-17).

CONCLUSION AND APPLICATION

Hebrews through Jude explain the newness of the new covenant, along with the abiding need to walk in obedience. Though we no longer live under the law as a covenant administration (which means we don't have to obey the ceremonial and civil aspects as such), the moral aspects of God's law remain binding. Christ accomplished salvation on our behalf, but believing in Christ requires that we live in a way that matches our confession (see Jas 2:14-26). These letters offer us blessings for obedience and warn about the curses that accrue to disobedience. Many of the applications from the previous chapter could be repeated here, but a few other aspects bear mention:

1. Jesus has really inaugurated the new covenant, but it is not yet here in its perfect fullness. This means that the present age is a mix of both blessing and difficulty. We really experience blessings in this age of fulfillment, yet opposition to Christ and his people remains. We therefore must not be surprised when the life of blessing is also the

life of persecution (see Mt 5:10-12; 1 Pet 3:14). We must persevere, continue to be warned against the sinfulness of our own hearts (Heb 3:13; see also Heb 3:19), and keep ourselves in the love of God (Jude 21). Though we are called actively to persevere, we do so in the light of God who watches over us and enables us every step of the way (2 Cor 13:14; Phil 1:6; Heb 13:20-21; Jude 24-25).

2. Jesus is coming again, and it matters how we live in the meantime. In 2 Peter the false teachers teach that since Jesus is not returning, our actions do not matter. Peter disagrees. Instead of indulging sinful desires, we should look ahead to the return of Christ and live righteous, godly lives as we look forward to the new heavens and the new earth (2 Pet 3:10-14).

Even so, we should remember that we are saved by grace and not by our actions. We can therefore look forward to the return of Christ as the day of salvation (Jas 5:7-8; 1 Pet 1:5, 7, 13; 1 Jn 2:28; 3:2; 4:17; Jude 21).

3. As we have seen throughout this study, obeying God's commands is not burdensome but is the way of blessing (e.g., Jas 1:25; 1 Jn 5:3). On the other hand, the path of sinfulness is the path of enslavement and destruction (Rom 6:6, 15-23; Gal 4:3, 8; Titus 3:3; 2 Pet 2:17-22; Jude 13-15). Let us pursue righteousness and not be deceived by the worldly spirit of this age.

SUGGESTED READING

Bauckham, Richard. *James*. NTR. London: Routledge, 1999.

Beale, G. K. *A New Testament Biblical Theology: The Unfolding of the Old Testament in the New*. Grand Rapids, MI: Baker Academic, 2011.

Crowe, Brandon D. *The Message of the General Epistles in the History of Redemption: Wisdom from James, Peter, John, and Jude*. Phillipsburg, NJ: P&R, 2015.

THE CONSUMMATION

THE BOOK OF REVELATION

I GREW UP WITH ONLY THREE *STAR WARS* MOVIES. This means there were many plot holes and questions that were never quite answered. In the first *Star Wars* (1977) Obi Wan Kenobi tells a young Luke Skywalker that a Jedi named Darth Vader betrayed and murdered his father. Three years later, in *The Empire Strikes Back*, Darth Vader memorably proclaims to Luke, "*I* am your father." Audiences had to wait three more years to find out whether Darth Vader really was Luke's father. In *Return of the Jedi* Obi Wan explains that Anakin Skywalker was seduced by the dark side and *became* Darth Vader, thus ("from a certain point of view") he did betray and murder Luke's father.

But I still had questions. Who was Anakin Skywalker? Why was he seduced by the dark side? How did he become part machine? Many of these questions were not answered on screen until years later, culminating in 2005's *Revenge of the Sith*—almost thirty years after the original *Star Wars*.

You've surely also anxiously anticipated the next installment of a book, a movie, or a TV series, hoping for loose ends to be wrapped up and lingering questions to be answered. Right now my own children are eager to discover who the mysterious "baby Yoda" of the *Star Wars* miniseries *The Mandalorian* is. Dangling plot lines build anticipation, and we long for resolution. Sometimes the ending is rewarding; other times we're left frustrated or confused. In this final chapter we come to the final book of the Bible: Revelation. Revelation fittingly concludes the biblical canon by echoing earlier Scripture, highlighting the completed work of Christ and sketching a vision for the future. Revelation wrestles with the ambiguities and difficulties of this age but doesn't leave the plot dangling. Revelation proclaims that Christ rules, and his people will be vindicated. Revelation is an immensely practical book that provides guidance for living today.

READING REVELATION

Since Revelation can be a difficult—and controversial—book, it will be helpful to discuss briefly how we ought to interpret it. Some view Revelation as a book of predictions. Certainly Revelation does speak about the future, but Revelation is much more than a book of predictions. Revelation casts a vision for life today. It calls God's people to covenant faithfulness. It warns us against sin and encourages us with the reality that "God rules history and will bring it to its consummation in Christ."[1] Revelation sets forth Jesus Christ as the risen and reigning King of kings, who calls his people to faith and perseverance. Revelation 17:14 helpfully sums up the thrust of the book: "They will make war on the Lamb, and the Lamb will conquer them, for he is Lord of lords and King of kings, and those with him are called and chosen and faithful."[2] We must not be swayed by the satanic spirit of this age, because God's purposes will ultimately prevail.[3]

It's crucial that we recognize and heed Revelation's calls to faithfulness in life. We go astray if we think of Revelation as a fatalistic book of predictions.

---

[1] Vern S. Poythress, *The Returning King: A Guide to the Book of Revelation* (Phillipsburg, NJ: P&R, 2000), 11.

[2] This verse is highlighted by William Hendriksen, *More Than Conquerors: An Interpretation of the Book of Revelation* (Grand Rapids, MI: Baker, 1967), 9.

[3] Compare also G. K. Beale, *The Book of Revelation: A Commentary on the Greek Text*, NIGTC (Grand Rapids, MI: Eerdmans, 1999), 33; Craig S. Keener, *Revelation*, NIVAC (Grand Rapids, MI: Zondervan, 1999), 43.

Revelation does not teach us to shut our eyes and sing "*Que Será, Será*" ("whatever will be, will be"). Instead, Revelation provides motivation for faithful covenant living in the present, in light of God's promises about the future.

This means Revelation is not only about the future; it's about the entire age of the church, from the first coming of Christ to his second coming. It doesn't focus only on the last few years of world history; it's about every era of the church's history. It's about things that are persistently true. As one helpful book on Revelation puts the matter, "[Revelation] is a book for every age. It is always up to date."[4]

Revelation is saturated with scriptural allusions. Often the key to interpreting Revelation comes from the Old Testament. In fact, when we encounter difficult questions in Revelation, the first place we ought to look is not to the current headlines but to the Old Testament (especially the Prophets). In Revelation John identifies the church as God's people and calls the church to practical holiness. Those who believe and obey will receive blessings, and those who turn their backs on God, curses. This is consistent with what we find throughout Scripture. Revelation also promises a blessing to those who hear and keep the word of God (Rev 1:3).

Be encouraged; though Revelation can be a difficult book to interpret, and we may not understand every passage, we can understand the big picture. And when we give attention to Revelation and heed its calls, we will be blessed.

NEW COVENANT IN REVELATION

Christ's present and future reign. Revelation opens with a vision of the glorious, resurrected Christ. This should guide our reading of Revelation. Already in the first century John saw Christ as the victorious King of kings. This is not something that's relegated only to the future but is true now. Jesus is the faithful witness, the firstborn from the dead (Rev 1:5), which brings to mind Jesus' faithfulness even in the face of death, and his vindication in his resurrection. This should encourage those who will similarly face trials in this world because of their confession of Jesus. Additionally, Jesus is the

---

[4]Hendriksen, *More Than Conquerors*, 29.

ruler of the kings of the earth (Rev 1:5), the risen King of kings and Lord of lords (Rev 17:14; 19:16). He is the promised king from David's line who has conquered death (Rev 5:5). He even shares the throne with God Almighty (e.g., Rev 4–5; 7:10, 17).[5]

The exalted picture of Jesus in Revelation is particularly encouraging when God's people face governments and powerful institutions aligned against them. Though it often seems like the world is stacked against God's people, Jesus has authority over all earthly powers, and his kingdom is the only one that lasts forever. Jesus will return in glory and will bring an end to those who oppose him (Rev 1:7; 7:9-17; 11:15-18; 15:2-4; 19:1-21). This kingdom is not something that will only be true in the future but has already begun now. Jesus has inaugurated the kingdom of God (e.g., Mt 4:17; Mk 1:15). The kingdom has not yet been perfected, or consummated (e.g., 1 Cor 15:24), but the kingdom will continue to grow until Christ returns (e.g., Mt 12:28; Acts 1:6, 8). Christ's kingdom grows not by military might, but by the faithful witness of God's people and the blood of the Lamb (Rev 12:11).

Christ is the ruler of the kings of the earth, and his people ought to live under his lordship now, for he is coming soon.

The church and true obedience. Similar to 1 Peter, in Revelation John speaks of the church as a kingdom and priests to God (Rev 1:6). As such God's people are distinct from the world and called to the holiness expressed by God's law.

This new covenant kingdom of priests does not comprise one ethnic people or those from within one geographical boundary. Instead, it's a worldwide people from every tribe, tongue, people, and nation (Rev 5:9-10; 7:9; 15:3-4; see also Rev 13:7; 20:6; 21:24; 22:2). Even where Revelation speaks of 144,000 people from the tribes of Israel, this is most likely a theological number that speaks of the fullness of God's people—including both Jews and Gentiles.

John addresses this fullness of God's people by writing to seven churches (Rev 1:4). Seven is another theological number that refers not only to seven discrete congregations (though these were real churches) but also represents

---

[5]Richard Bauckham, *The Theology of the Book of Revelation*, NTT (Cambridge: Cambridge University Press, 1993), 54-65.

the totality of the church in the present age.[6] The seven churches John addresses are a mixed bag (see Rev 2–3). Some are doing well (Smyrna, Philadelphia); some are not doing well (Ephesus, Laodicea); and some were a mixture of good and bad (Pergamum, Thyatira, Sardis).[7] In his exhortations to each congregation, John focuses consistently on the role of the church in the midst of a pagan society.[8] Much like Revelation as a whole, each letter in Revelation 2–3 speaks of the glories of Christ and calls for faithfulness in light of the promises of God.

Most of the churches are encouraged in what they are doing well (only Laodicea is not). We have much to learn from Christ's approbations. Christ encourages the church in Ephesus for its perseverance and theological fidelity in spite of difficulty (Rev 2:2-3, 6). The Smyrneans and Philadelphians face opposition for their confession of faith from those of Jewish heritage who claim to be God's people but who have not embraced Jesus as Messiah (in Smyrna and Philadelphia in Rev 2:9; 3:8-10). This persecution God's people faced, however, is not a sign of God's displeasure. These difficulties should not be construed as covenantal curses for disobedience but are actually results of their faithfulness. They must persevere (Rev 2:10; 3:10). The church at Pergamum has resisted idolatry (Rev 2:13), and the church at Thyatira is commended for faith, love, and perseverance (Rev 2:19). In Sardis is a remnant who has not soiled its clothes, presumably with the sinfulness of the world (Rev 3:4). These commendations guide us today in the way of righteousness in the midst of an ungodly world.

John's letters also include warnings to five of the seven churches (Smyrna and Philadelphia are excluded). The Ephesians are rebuked for neglecting their first love (Rev 2:4). This first love most likely refers to the Ephesians' coldness toward those around them, violating the second great command (see Lev 19:18).[9] Similarly, it appears that the church in Sardis has expired

---

[6]"Muratorian Fragment," in Edmon L. Gallagher and John D. Meade, *The Biblical Canon Lists from Early Christianity: Texts and Analysis* (Oxford: Oxford University Press, 2017), 180 (lines 58-60); Hendriksen, *More Than Conquerors*, 16; Dennis E. Johnson, *The Triumph of the Lamb: A Commentary on Revelation* (Phillipsburg, NJ: P&R, 2001), 69.

[7]Beale, *Revelation*, 226.

[8]So Beale, *Revelation*, 227.

[9]See also Johnson, *Triumph*, 72.

in its witness to those around them (Rev 3:1-2).[10] The Laodiceans are rebuked for self-reliance (Rev 3:17-18).

Christ also rebukes several churches for tolerating sexual immorality. The church in Pergamum holds to the teaching of Balaam, recalling the false prophet who seduced the Israelites in the Old Testament with idolatry and sexual immorality (see Num 22–24). Likewise, the church in Pergamum is rebuked for its participation in idolatry and sexual immorality (Rev 2:14-15), and the church in Thyatira is rebuked for tolerating Jezebel, who promotes idolatry and sexual immorality (Rev 2:20). One of the ways that sexual immorality may have been promoted is through participation in professional societies, or trade guilds, which involved idolatrous and sexually illicit activities.[11] If so, it seems likely that false teachers were promoting participation in these activities, perhaps in the name of "relevance." But John warns of the danger of such activities. They are not *adiaphora*—things that don't really matter—but they matter a great deal. Though abstaining from such professional societies may have led to social and economic hardships, it is not appropriate for God's holy people to indulge in idolatry and sexual immorality.

It's important to recognize that John addresses covenant communities, and that one's identity as a member of God's people does not necessarily ensure faithfulness (e.g., Rev 3:19). Not all those in the covenant community are faithful covenant members. And sometimes even true covenant members go astray. God's covenant people are called to obey his commands (Rev 12:17; 14:12). When God's covenant people turn away from his commands, they must be warned to repent. Since Jesus is the King of all kings, we must hold fast to his commands, showing him fealty. The true child of God is the one who overcomes the world (Rev 21:7). Repentance is a mark of true believers (contrast Rev 9:20-21). There is more to life than the here-and-now of self-indulgence; those who cling to the Lamb and to his commands will be saved (see Rev 14:4-5). Revelation by no means teaches salvation by our works (see Rev 1:5; 5:9; 7:14; 12:11), but it does teach that God's people must walk in obedience and repentance.[12]

---

[10]See Beale, *Revelation*, 273.

[11]This seems especially relevant for Pergamum and Thyatira; See Beale, *Revelation*, 261.

[12]Note the emphasis on overcoming or conquering, e.g., Rev 2:7, 11, 17, 26; 3:5, 12, 21; 12:11; 15:2; 21:7.

In short, Revelation teaches that true Christians are "those who keep the commandments of God and their faith in Jesus" (Rev 14:12).

Conflict in this age. The calls to persevere in faith in Revelation are clarion because of the reality that there will be conflict between those who profess Christ and the world. Revelation shows that behind conflicts on a local scale lies a spiritual conflict of cosmic proportions. This is recounted in the central section of Revelation (Rev 12–14). The great dragon, the devil (Rev 12:3, 9), comes after the messianic child (see Rev 12:5). However, the child is protected and caught up to heaven; the devil's attacks have failed. This passage focuses on the incarnation and victorious work of Christ over the devil—from his birth, to his death, to his resurrection and ascension (esp. Rev 12:5, 7-9).[13] As John says elsewhere, Jesus came to destroy the works of the devil (1 Jn 3:8). Moses conquered the giant Og, and David toppled Goliath. But Jesus triumphs over the spiritual authorities in the heavenly places (see Eph 1:20-21; 3:10) and the devil himself. When Jesus defeats the dragon, the devil turns and attacks the people of God (Rev 12:6, 13-17). The people of God are protected and are identified by their pattern of life—they keep the commandments of God (Rev 12:17). This again reveals the holiness that must be characteristic of God's true people.

The devil fails to defeat the Messiah, and he will not succeed in wiping out the people of God (see Rev 11:7-13). Nevertheless, the devil comes after God's people with his own servants. Revelation 13:1-10 speaks of a fierce beast from the sea, representing earthly power structures who do the bidding of the dragon (Rev 13:1-4). The beast from the sea makes war against God's people and exerts significant pressure and violence on them for forty-two months (Rev 13:4-5, 7, 10). A second beast arises from the earth and serves as the mouthpiece for the beast from the sea (Rev 13:11-18). The beast from the land would deceive us into worshiping the beast from the sea (Rev 13:14), and together the dragon and the two beasts serve as something like an unholy Trinity seeking to turn people away from the true and living God.[14]

Revelation teaches God's covenant people what to expect in this age. Much like Peter exhorts us not to be surprised at the fiery trial (1 Pet 4:12),

---

[13]See Beale, *Revelation*, 639, 650-56.
[14]See Poythress, *Returning King*, 16-18.

in Revelation John teaches that the opposition to God's people has already begun. The tribulation is not a period relegated to the future; John himself already shares in the tribulation (Rev 1:9). Unfortunately, many mistakenly believe that Revelation teaches the church is spared the persecution. This sets us up for great disappointment. The Scriptures don't promise the church that it will be spared persecution. Jesus and Paul experienced tribulation, and both warn that tribulations will come in this age (e.g., Mt 10:24-25; Acts 14:22; 2 Tim 3:12; see also 1 Pet 2:21). Revelation teaches the same thing. Some from the church in Smyrna will be thrown into prison for a short time, but the call is to be faithful even unto death (Rev 2:9-10; 7:14). In Revelation the church participates in the tribulation and is marginalized by the world. Yet it only lasts forty-two months, which shows us that it's a limited period, only half of the fullness of seven years.[15] God is in control.

Persecution won't last forever, for even persecution is under the control of God. Throughout Revelation judgments fall on those who "dwell on the earth," which refers specifically to unbelievers who disobey God's law (e.g., Rev 3:10; 6:10; 8:13; 11:10; 13:14; 14:6). In contrast, the judgments do not ultimately harm those who worship the Lamb. They are sealed and protected (Rev 7:1-8; 14:1-5).

"Here is a call," says Revelation 13:10, for the perseverance of the saints: life in this world will be difficult, but there will be blessings for those who persevere in faith and cling fast to the commandments of God (Rev 14:12). We should be sober, but also encouraged because Jesus has already defeated the dragon. Though the authorities of this age align against Jesus and his people, Jesus will overcome all opposition as the King of kings (Rev 17:14). Though the rulers of this age may seem powerful; though it seems there is no way we can resist the beast, yet they will all be destroyed. Kingdoms arrayed against Jesus and his people will become like a ghost town—a haunt for jackals (Rev 18:2). They will be destroyed quickly and definitively, and those who have been clinging to them will have nowhere to hide (Rev 6:15-17; 18:9-10, 15, 19). Despite the difficulty facing God's people in this age,

---

[15]Poythress, *Returning King*, 127; see also Beale, *Revelation*, 565-68.

perseverance in the face of hostility is worth it. For we serve the ruler of the kings of the earth (Rev 1:5; see also Rev 2:10, 26).

NEW JERUSALEM

John further casts a vision for the holiness of God's people by describing the consummate state as one of purity, holiness, and safety from all enemies. This brings us to the final two chapters of Revelation (Rev 21–22), which speak of a reality even greater than the one in the opening chapters of Scripture. Revelation 21–22 speak about the consummation of God's kingdom—the new heaven and the new earth (Rev 21:1), with particular focus on the new Jerusalem (Rev 21:2).[16] Just as God created the world in the beginning, so in the future will he restore and renew the world (see Is 65:17; Mt 19:28; Acts 3:21; Rom 8:21-22; 2 Pet 3:5-13).[17] This will be a world of righteousness and glory, free from sin and conflict. Covenant blessings will abound, and the covenant curses will be banished from God's presence. God's true covenant people will be free to obey God fully.

This new world, which is described like a temple, will be characterized by close fellowship with God. In the beginning Eden is described as a temple in the midst of God's creation—a holy place of God's special presence, whose borders were to be expanded to fill the whole earth.[18] In Eden God walked with Adam and Eve as their covenantal God. This vision was echoed in the Promised Land, which was to be a holy land of fellowship between God and his people. The special presence of God was focused and set forth in a special way in the tabernacle and later in the temple.

The new Jerusalem provides a place of close, covenantal fellowship with God and his people—this is what Eden, the Promised land, the tabernacle, and the temple were all designed to support. The city is like a bride prepared for her husband (Rev 21:2, 9). Once the city descends, it is the place of God's covenantal presence with his people—he dwells among his people as their God (Rev 21:3, 7). There is no separate temple in the New Jerusalem, for the Lord God almighty and the Lamb are the temple (Rev 21:22). This points to

---

[16]Poythress, *Returning King*, 185-86; see also Beale, *Revelation*, 1109-10.
[17]See Poythress, *Returning King*, 185.
[18]See Beale, *Revelation*, 1111.

the immediacy and intimacy of covenant fellowship with God in the consummate state (see Rev 22:4-5).[19] The cubic dimensions of the new Jerusalem (Rev 21:16) recall the dimensions of the holy of holies and Ezekiel's temple (Ezek 40–48): the whole city is a temple where God will dwell with his people.[20] Nor is there any need for a sun, for the glory of God and the light of the Lamb surpasses the glory of the sun (Rev 21:23). This will be a world of great joy.

The end of Revelation is also clear about who participates in these consummate blessings. The blessings are for those who overcome the world, who cling to the Lamb and his commandments (Rev 21:7; see also Rev 12:17; 14:12). The new Jerusalem is a holy place. No one can earn their way in, but those who inhabit it reflect the character of the Lamb. Those excluded include "the cowardly, the faithless, the detestable . . . murderers, the sexually immoral, sorcerers, idolaters, and all liars" (Rev 21:8; see similarly Rev 22:15). This list closely reflects statements from Paul and other New Testament authors and confirms that our actions matter. Instead of experiencing the blessings of eternal life, the place of those described in Revelation 21:8 is the lake of fire, the second death. This place of ultimate cursing has no place in the new Jerusalem in the new heaven and new earth.

The new Jerusalem is a city of purity, reserved for those whose names are written in the Lamb's book of life (Rev 21:27) and who walk in his ways. The expulsion of the wicked also speaks to the security of this new city (see Rev 21:27; 22:3).[21] It is a massive city (twelve thousand cubits—about fourteen hundred miles—long, Rev 21:16) with plenty of room.[22] It is a beautiful city (Rev 21:11, 18-21; see also Rev 21:2) with enormous walls that, like the gates, represent the fullness of the people of God (Rev 21:17).[23] At the same time, the gates are always open (Rev 21:25). There is no danger nor is there night, for the light of God shines without ceasing (Rev 21:23-27). Unlike our world, night never comes. It will be perpetual day. Sin has no home here.

---

[19]See Hendriksen, *More Than Conquerors*, 203.

[20]Beale, *Revelation*, 1073; G. K. Beale, *The Temple and the Church's Mission: A Biblical Theology of the Dwelling Place of God*, NSBT 17 (Downers Grove, IL: InterVarsity Press, 2004), 23-25, 366-73.

[21]See Beale, *Revelation*, 1072, 1091.

[22]See Poythress, *Returning King*, 191.

[23]See Hendriksen, *More Than Conquerors*, 202; Beale, *Revelation*, 1070, 1076; Johnson, *Triumph*, 310.

THE CONSUMMATION OF THE COVENANTS

As we conclude this study of the whole Bible, it may be helpful to explain briefly how Revelation shows the final fulfillment of the preceding biblical covenants: Adam, Noah, Abraham, Moses, David, and the new covenant.

In the beginning Adam had a goal in front of him—the possibility for everlasting, glorious life. The final chapter of the Bible recalls the beginning of the Bible and the prospect of life. The Garden of Eden contained the tree of life, and from Eden flowed a river that brought life to the surrounding lands (Gen 2:10-14). Ezekiel speaks of life-giving waters flowing from God's temple, which makes sense because Eden is also portrayed as a temple (Ezek 47:1-12).[24] In Revelation the river of the water of life flows from the throne (Rev 22:1-2; see also Rev 21:6). This recalls not only God's original creation, but also the life that Jesus himself gives (Jn 7:37-38). At the same time, there is no sea (Rev 21:1) The sea represents chaos and opposition to God; the lack of a sea points to peace in the new age.[25]

On either side of the life-giving water in the new Jerusalem stands the tree of life (Rev 22:2). The tree of life was present with Adam in the beginning. In Revelation it returns, for the last Adam has obeyed perfectly and offers life to all who trust in him. Jesus secures the eternal life that Adam did not. The instability of the covenant of works with Adam—Adam was in a probationary state by which he could have sinned or not sinned; he was not yet in possession of glorious, eternal life—has been overcome by the work of Christ in the covenant of grace.[26] Christ has secured eternal life. In the new Jerusalem the tree of life bears twelve kinds of fruits for the healing of the nations (Rev 22:2). Those who overcome—who have been purified by the blood of the Lamb—receive the right to eat of the tree of life (Rev 2:7; 22:14; see also Rev 22:19).

The stability of the new creation recalls God's Covenant with Noah. The new creation will last forever. Further, the rainbow reappears in Revelation

---

[24]See Beale, *Revelation*, 1104-5.

[25]Note also the beast who comes out of the sea in Rev 13:1-10, recalling the beastly kingdoms of Daniel 7:2-8. See also Beale, *Revelation*, 683-703, 1042.

[26]Bavinck, *RD*, 3:406; Turretin, *Inst.* 8.1.7 (1:570); Geerhardus Vos, "The Doctrine of the Covenant in Reformed Theology," in *Redemptive History and Biblical Interpretation: The Shorter Writings of Geerhardus Vos*, ed. Richard B. Gaffin Jr. (Phillipsburg, NJ: P&R, 1980), 257-58.

around God's throne (Rev 4:3; see also Rev 10:1), reminding God's people of his mercy, as in the days of Noah.[27]

Fulfilling the promise to Abraham of a land are the permanence and security of the new heavens and new earth. Additionally, this new creation is filled with people from every tribe, tongue, people, and nation (e.g., Rev 5:9-10; 7:9; 15:3-4), thus showing that God has fulfilled his promise to Abraham to bless all the nations of the earth through him (Gen 12:1-3). This is possible through Jesus Christ, the true Son of Abraham.

The Mosaic covenant also speaks of a land of promise, especially by means of the law given to them that they might dwell with God permanently in covenantal fellowship. In the new heavens and new earth unrighteousness is banished (Rev 21:8). The kingship promised to David is fulfilled in Jesus Christ, the ruler not only over David's dynasty (Rev 3:7; 5:5; 22:16) but the ruler of all the kings of the earth (Rev 1:5). His kingdom lasts forever, and those found in him will reign with him (Rev 22:5).

Finally, Revelation also pictures the consummation of the new covenant. Like the Last Supper, the marriage supper of the lamb (Rev 19:7-10) is a covenant meal celebrated in the presence of Jesus himself. Yet this meal is not one of anticipation, but of consummation; it is the meal to which Jesus looked forward in the Last Supper (see Mt 26:29). This meal anticipates the consummation when the church is finally presented as the bride of the Lamb (Rev 21:9).[28] The Lamb emerges victorious in the end.

As with all biblical covenants, the end result is doxology: praise to the God of Scripture (Rev 22:9). Here Revelation ends, reminding us that Jesus is coming soon; blessed are those who keep his commandments (Rev 22:7-9).

CONCLUSION AND APPLICATION

The end is better than the beginning. In the beginning Adam existed in a state of uncertainty, with the prospect of eternal life held out before him. Adam did not realize the goal before him by upholding his end of the covenant. But in Revelation we see the wonderful reality that what Adam could not do, Jesus did. Eternal life has been secured by the perfect covenant mediator, and

---

[27]Beale, *Revelation*, 321.
[28]Johnson, *Triumph*, 263.

he offers it freely to sinners. Even so, those who follow the Lamb must keep the commandments. This is not a new perspective but echoes the Scriptures from first to last. In Revelation the resolution comes as the devil and evil are finally banished and God's people are free to live according to the light of his law, in fellowship with him, forever.

As we look forward to this consummation, Revelation urges us toward covenant faithfulness in the present age in many ways.

1. God rules world history. Though followers of Jesus will face difficulty in this age, this does not mean that God does not see or God is not in control. Though for a season it seems like opposition to God may prevail, in the end God and his people will be vindicated. The plagues that affect humanity are under God's control, and his purposes will ultimately prevail. Revelation provides us a peek behind the curtain to show us there is more going on than meets the eye. What we don't find in the daily news we find in Revelation: Jesus is the true victor, and his often-marginalized people will reign with him (Rev 5:10; 20:4, 6; 22:5). When we look around us and all seems lost, Revelation encourages us to persevere and remember that Jesus is coming soon.

2. God will fulfill his covenant promises. The new heaven and the new earth fulfill the promise to Abraham and his descendants that they would inherit the world (see Rev 5:13). Eternal life is the fulfillment of the covenantal promises to the patriarchs, who did not receive all that was promised to them in their lifetimes (see Ex 3:6; Lk 20:37-38; Heb 11:13). The eternal life offered to Adam in the covenant of works, represented by the tree of life, is granted through faith in Jesus Christ. The kingdom promised to David has become a reality through Jesus, the resurrected king over all kings (Rev 1:5; 17:14; 19:16; see also 2 Sam 7:13; Lk 1:32-33).

3. Jesus is the glorious Lord of lords who reigns over all kings. Jesus is not simply one religious teacher among many; he is unique as the one who is truly God and truly man. There is no other mediator between God and man. No one else has made atonement for sin and shares the throne with God the Father. In Jesus' first coming, he came in

humiliation. Yet this is not the appropriate way to think of Jesus' present state. Revelation shows us that Jesus has now entered his state of glory, and no one can stand against him. The suffering and death that Jesus experienced in his state of humiliation have been overcome and now he lives and reigns forever. He calls for faith and obedience, and he promises final victory for all who follow him.

4. It pays to persevere. Often the church in this age faces difficulty for its faith. At times it may seem pointless or futile to resist the spirit of the age. Are we alone? Does anyone else care about God's law? When we look around, it often seems like immorality and injustice reign. But Revelation encourages us that God has not forgotten, and God sees all. The righteous will be comforted, and the wicked who reject God and his law will be judged. It therefore matters whom we worship and how we live (Rev 22:12).

5. Jesus is coming back. And he is coming soon. Blessed are the servants whom the Lord finds doing his will when he returns (Lk 12:37, 43). Since Jesus is coming soon, "let the one who does right continue to do right; and let the holy person continue to be holy" (Rev 22:11 NIV).

SUGGESTED READING

Bauckham, Richard. *The Theology of the Book of Revelation*. Cambridge: Cambridge University Press, 1993.

Beale, G. K. and David Campbell. *Revelation: A Shorter Commentary*. Grand Rapids, MI: Eerdmans, 2015.

Hendriksen, William. *More Than Conquerors: An Interpretation of the Book of Revelation*. Grand Rapids, MI: Baker, 1967.

Johnson, Dennis E. *The Triumph of the Lamb: A Commentary on Revelation*. Phillipsburg, NJ: P&R, 2001.

Poythress, Vern S. *The Returning King: A Guide to the Book of Revelation*. Phillipsburg, NJ: P&R, 2000.

CONCLUSION:
GRACE UPON GRACE

THE BIBLE IS A BEAUTIFUL, UNIFIED BOOK, and it focuses on a beautiful Savior. Central to the storyline of Scripture are God's promises to walk among his people and bless them as their God. Along with this, he calls his people to live faithfully in covenant with him. Though this can become complex, it is quite straightforward at its root. God is the king who desires fellowship with his people. And this fellowship comes on his terms. Despite all the progression and advancement toward the final goal of Christ and his consummate kingdom we find in Scripture, God's people are never freed *from* obedience. God remains king over us. Instead, in the new covenant era we are freed from the dominion of the law and empowered by the Holy Spirit in a new way to fulfill the righteous requirements of the law.

At the same time, the grandness of the new covenant does not mean that the old covenant is inherently bad or that Old Testament believers were somehow saved in a fundamentally different way. All people who have been saved have been saved by grace, and obedience has always been the appropriate response of God's people to his beneficence. This does not change in the New Testament.

In the introduction I summarized four key points. I repeat them here, with a few comments.

1. All people are obligated to obey their Creator. The God of the Bible is not simply the God of one people; he is the God of the whole world. He made from one man every nation on the face of the earth (Acts 17:26). It doesn't matter a person's background or origin; all people are obligated to the Creator of the world who has appointed one man to be the judge of the whole world (Acts 17:30-31). The proper response is faith and repentance.

2. God freely entered into a covenant with humanity to offer eternal life on the basis of perfect obedience. This was true with Adam and remains true today—eternal life requires perfect obedience. Further, every person relates to God either in Adam or in Christ. To be in Adam means to be characterized by the way of works that leads to death. To be in Christ means living by faith in the One whose perfect obedience leads to everlasting life. All who are in Christ are heirs of wonderfully rich covenantal promises.

3. Only Jesus can perfectly obey God's law. There is nothing we can do to earn eternal life. If we are to inherit eternal life, we must place our faith in Christ whose obedience meets the requirement of perfect obedience for eternal life.

4. The law continues to show us how to obey God today. Though our obedience is always imperfect, even imperfect obedience brings great blessing for those in Christ. Though we cannot meet the requirements for eternal life, we are not exonerated from obedience. Love and obedience go hand in hand as we walk in covenant fellowship with our covenant Lord. Moreover, the way of obedience to God's law continues to be the way of blessing. This is, to be sure, a radically countercultural message, but it is a deeply biblical message.

We end where the Gospel of John begins: with the riches of blessings that come from Jesus. "For from his fullness we have all received, and grace in place of grace. For the law was given through Moses; grace and truth came through Jesus Christ" (Jn 1:16-17, my translation). John does not speak of a fundamental difference between the Old and New Testaments, as though there was no grace given through Moses. The days of Moses were days of grace. The law given through Moses was a great blessing for God's people. It reveals his character and guides God's covenant people in the ways of life. The law given through Moses was a good and gracious thing. Grace and law are not antithetical in the context of the covenant.

Yet Jesus brings a better day of grace. Whereas Moses could only mediate the law, we receive grace and truth from Jesus himself. He grants abundant life to all who will come to him. And when we do, we find a Savior who shows us the way of life that is both new and old: the old path of obedience to God's law that has been required from the beginning and a new path that he has walked perfectly, yielding salvation for all who trust in him.

Jesus shows us that obedience to God's law should be our delight, for this is the path of fellowship with our covenant Lord.

BIBLIOGRAPHY

Alexander, T. D. *From Paradise to the Promised Land: An Introduction to the Pentateuch*. 2nd ed. Grand Rapids, MI: Baker Academic, 2002.

Allison, Dale C., Jr. "Mark 12:28-31 and the Decalogue." In *The Gospels and the Scriptures of Israel*, edited by Craig A. Evans and W. Richard Stegner, 270-78. JSNT Sup 104 / SSEJC 3. Sheffield: Sheffield Academic Press, 1994.

_____. "Structure, Biographical Impulse, and the *Imitatio Christi*." In *Studies in Matthew: Interpretation Past and Present*, 135-55. Grand Rapids, MI: Baker Academic, 2005.

Baldwin, Joyce G. *Daniel: An Introduction and Commentary*. TOTC 23. Downers Grove, IL: InterVarsity Press, 1978.

Barker, Kenneth L. and Waylon Bailey. *Micah, Nahum, Habakkuk, Zephaniah*. NAC 20. Nashville: Broadman & Holman, 1999.

Bauckham, Richard. *James*. NTR. London: Routledge, 1999.

_____. *The Theology of the Book of Revelation*. NTT. Cambridge: Cambridge University Press, 1993.

Baugh, S. M. *Ephesians*. EEC. Bellingham, WA: Lexham Press, 2016.

Bavinck, Herman. *Reformed Dogmatics*. Edited by John Bolt. Translated by John Vriend. 4 vols. Grand Rapids, MI: Baker Academic, 2003–8.

_____. *The Wonderful Works of God: Instruction in the Christian Religion According to the Reformed Confession*. Translated by Henry Zylstra (1956). With a new introduction by R. Calrton Wynne. Philadelphia: Westminster Seminary Press, 2019.

Beale, G. K. *A New Testament Biblical Theology: The Unfolding of the Old Testament in the New*. Grand Rapids, MI: Baker Academic, 2011.

————. *The Book of Revelation: A Commentary on the Greek Text*. NIGTC. Grand Rapids, MI: Eerdmans, 1999.

————. *The Morality of God in the Old Testament*. CAHQ. Phillipsburg, NJ: P&R, 2013.

Beale, G. K. and D. A. Carson, eds. *Commentary on the New Testament Use of the Old Testament*. Grand Rapids, MI: Baker Academic, 2007.

Beale, G. K. and David Campbell. *Revelation: A Shorter Commentary*. Grand Rapids, MI: Eerdmans, 2015.

Belcher, Richard P., Jr. *The Fulfillment of the Promises of God: An Explanation of Covenant Theology*. Fearn, Ross-shire: Mentor, 2020.

————. "The Covenant of Works in the Old Testament." In *Covenant Theology: Biblical, Theological, and Historical Perspectives*, edited by Guy Prentiss Waters, J. Nicholas Reid, and John R. Muether. 63-78. Wheaton, IL: Crossway, 2020.

Berkhof, Louis. *Systematic Theology*. 4th ed. Grand Rapids, MI: Eerdmans, 1996.

Block, Daniel I. *Deuteronomy*. NIVAC. Grand Rapids, MI: Zondervan, 2012.

————. *Judges, Ruth*. NAC 6. Nashville: Broadman & Holman, 1999.

Bruce, F. F. *Romans*. 2nd ed. TNTC. Grand Rapids, MI: Eerdmans, 1985.

Calvin, John. *Commentaries on the First Book of Moses Called Genesis*. Translated by John King. 2 vols. 1923. Reprint, Grand Rapids, MI: Baker, 2003.

————. *Institutes of the Christian Religion*. Edited by John T. McNeill. Translated by Ford Lewis Battles. 2 vols. LCC 20–21. Louisville, KY: Westminster John Knox, 1960.

Carson, D. A. *The Farewell Discourse and the Final Prayer of Jesus: An Evangelical Exposition of John 14–17*. Grand Rapids, MI: Baker, 1980.

Childs, Brevard S. *Isaiah: A Commentary*. OTL. Louisville, KY: Westminster John Knox, 2001.

Clements, R. E. *God's Chosen People: A Theological Introduction of the Book of Deuteronomy*. London: SCM, 1968.

Coxhead, Steven R. "The Cardionomographic Work of the Spirit in the Old Testament." *WTJ* 79 (2017): 77-95.

Craigie, Peter C. *The Book of Deuteronomy*. NICOT. Grand Rapids, MI: Eerdmans, 1976.

Crowe, Brandon D. *The Hope of Israel: The Resurrection of Christ in the Acts of the Apostles*. Grand Rapids, MI: Baker Academic, 2020.

————. *The Last Adam: A Theology of the Obedient Life of Jesus in the Gospels*. Grand Rapids, MI: Baker Academic, 2017.

————. *The Message of the General Epistles in the History of Redemption: Wisdom from James, Peter, John, and Jude*. Phillipsburg, NJ: P&R, 2015.

————. *The Obedient Son: Deuteronomy and Christology in the Gospel of Matthew*. BZNW 188. Berlin: de Gruyter, 2012.

_____. "The Passive and Active Obedience of Christ: Retrieving a Biblical Distinction." In *The Doctrine on which the Church Stands or Falls: Justification in Biblical, Theological, Historical, and Pastoral Perspective*, edited by Matthew Barrett, 437-64. Wheaton, IL: Crossway, 2019.

Davies, W. D. and Dale C. Allison, Jr., *A Critical and Exegetical Commentary on the Gospel According to St. Matthew*. 3 vols. ICC. Edinburgh: T&T Clark, 1988–97.

Davis, Dale Ralph. *1 Kings: The Wisdom and the Folly*. Fearn, Ross-Shire: Christian Focus, 2002.

_____. *2 Samuel: Out of Every Adversity*. Fearn, Ross-Shire: Christian Focus, 1999.

_____. *Judges: Such a Great Salvation*. Fearn, Ross-Shire: Christian Focus, 2000.

Dempster, Stephen G. *Dominion and Dynasty: A Theology of the Hebrew Bible*. NSBT 15. Downers Grove, IL: InterVarsity Press, 2003.

DeYoung, Kevin. *The Ten Commandments: What They Mean, Why They Matter, and Why We Should Obey Them*. Wheaton, IL: Crossway, 2018.

Dumbrell, William J. *Covenant and Creation: A Theology of Old Testament Covenants*. Grand Rapids, MI: Baker, 1993.

Eichrodt, Walter. *Theology of the Old Testament*. Translated by J. Baker. 2 vols. OTL. London: SCM Press, 1961–67.

Ferguson, Sinclair B. *The Holy Spirit*. CCT. Downers Grove, IL: InterVarsity Press, 1996.

_____. *The Sermon on the Mount*. Edinburgh: Banner of Truth, 1987.

_____. *The Whole Christ: Legalism, Antinomianism, and Gospel Assurance—Why the Marrow Controversy Still Matters*. Wheaton, IL: Crossway, 2016.

France, R. T. *The Gospel of Matthew*. NICNT. Grand Rapids, MI: Eerdmans, 2007.

Gaffin, Richard B., Jr. *By Faith, Not by Sight: Paul and the Order of Salvation*. Waynesboro, GA: Paternoster, 2006.

Gallagher, Edmon L., and John D. Meade. *The Biblical Canon Lists from Early Christianity: Texts and Analysis*. Oxford: Oxford University Press, 2017.

Gladd, Benjamin L. *From Adam and Israel to the Church: A Biblical Theology of the People of God*. ESBT. Downers Grove, IL: IVP Academic, 2019.

Gonzales, Robert R., Jr. "Faults of Our Fathers: The Spread of Sin in the Patriarchal Narratives and its Implications." *WTJ* 74 (2012): 367-86.

Goodwin, Thomas. *Christ Set Forth*. Vol. 4 of *The Works of Thomas Goodwin*. Edinburgh: James Nicol, 1862.

Green, Bradley G. *Covenant and Commandment: Works, Obedience, and Faithfulness in the Christian Life*. NSBT 33. Downers Grove, IL: InterVarsity Press, 2014.

Harriman, James Earl. "Our Father in Heaven: The Dimensions of Divine Paternity in Deuteronomy." PhD diss., The Southern Baptist Theological Seminary, 2005.

Harrison, R. K. *Jeremiah and Lamentations: An Introduction and Commentary.* TOTC 21. Nottingham: Inter-Varsity, 1973.

Hays, Richard B. *The Moral Vision of the New Testament—Community, Cross, New Creation: A Contemporary Introduction to New Testament Ethics.* San Francisco: Harper, 1996.

Hendriksen, William. *More Than Conquerors: An Interpretation of the Book of Revelation.* Grand Rapids, MI: Baker, 1967.

Holmes, Michael W. *The Apostolic Fathers: Greek Texts and English Translations.* 3rd ed. Grand Rapids, MI: Baker Academic, 2007.

Howard, David M., Jr. *Joshua.* NAC 5. Nashville: Broadman & Holman, 1998.

Hugenberger, Gordon Paul. *Marriage as Covenant: A Study of Biblical Law and Ethics Governing Marriage Developed from the Perspective of Malachi.* VTSup 52. Leiden: Brill, 1994.

Johnson, Dennis E. "The Function of Romans 7:13-25 in Paul's Argument for the Law's Impotence and the Spirit's Power, and Its Bearing on the Schizophrenic 'I.'" In *Resurrection and Eschatology: Theology in the Service of the Church. Essays in Honor of Richard B. Gaffin, Jr.*, edited by Lane G. Tipton and Jeffrey C. Waddington, 3-59. Phillipsburg, NJ: P&R, 2008.

———. *The Triumph of the Lamb: A Commentary on Revelation.* Phillipsburg, NJ: P&R, 2001.

———. *Walking with Jesus Through His Word: Discovering Christ in All the Scriptures.* Phillipsburg, NJ: P&R, 2015.

Keener, Craig S. *Revelation.* NIVAC. Grand Rapids, MI: Zondervan, 1999.

———. *A Socio-Rhetorical Commentary on the Gospel According to Matthew.* Grand Rapids, MI: Eerdmans, 2009.

Kistemaker, Simon J. *Exposition of the Epistles of Peter and the Epistle of Jude.* NTC. Grand Rapids, MI: Baker Book House, 1987.

Kline, Meredith G. *Kingdom Prologue.* Overland Park, KS: Two Age Press, 2000.

Kruse, Colin G. *Paul's Letter to the Romans*, PNTC. Grand Rapids, MI: Eerdmans, 2012.

Lane, William L. *Hebrews.* WBC 47A–B. Nashville: Thomas Nelson, 1991–2000.

LaRondelle, Hans K. *The Israel of God in Prophecy: Principles of Prophetic Interpretation.* Berrien Springs, MI: Andrews University Press, 1983.

Letham, Robert. *A Christian's Pocket Guide to Baptism.* Fearn, Ross-Shire: Christian Focus, 2012.

Lincoln, Andrew T. *Ephesians.* WBC 42. Nashville: Thomas Nelson, 1990.

McCartney, Dan G. *James.* BECNT. Grand Rapids, MI: Baker Academic, 2009.

Moo, Douglas J. *The Letter of James.* PNTC. Grand Rapids, MI: Eerdmans, 2000.

Morales, L. Michael. *Who Shall Ascend the Mountain of the Lord? A Biblical Theology of the Book of Leviticus.* NSBT 37. Downers Grove, IL: InterVarsity Press, 2015.

Moran, William L. "The Ancient Near Eastern Background of the Love of God in Deuteronomy." *CBQ* 25 (1963): 77-87.

Murray, John. *Christian Baptism.* Phillipsburg, NJ: P&R, 1980.

_____. *The Epistle to the Romans.* 2 vols. NICNT. Grand Rapids, MI: Eerdmans, 1959–65.

_____. *Principles of Conduct: Aspects of Biblical Ethics.* Grand Rapids, MI: Eerdmans, 1957.

_____. *Redemption Accomplished and Applied.* Grand Rapids, MI: Eerdmans, 1955.

Pennington, Jonathan T. *The Sermon on the Mount and Human Flourishing: A Theological Commentary.* Grand Rapids, MI: Baker Academic, 2017.

Poythress, Vern S. *The Miracles of Jesus: How the Savior's Mighty Acts Serve as Signs of Redemption.* Wheaton, IL: Crossway, 2016.

_____. *The Returning King: A Guide to the Book of Revelation.* Phillipsburg, NJ: P&R, 2000.

_____. *The Shadow of Christ in the Law of Moses.* Phillipsburg, NJ: P&R, 1991.

Pratt, Richard L., Jr. "Out with the Old and in with the New." *TableTalk* 38.5 (2014): 12-15.

Quarles, Charles. *Sermon on the Mount: Restoring Christ's Message to the Modern Church.* NACSBT. Nashville: B&H Publishing, 2011.

Redd, John Scott. "The Abrahamic Covenant." In *Covenant Theology: Biblical, Theological, and Historical Perspectives*, edited by Guy Prentiss Waters, J. Nicholas Reid, and John R. Muether, 133-47. Wheaton, IL: Crossway, 2020.

Rhodes, Jonty. *Covenants Made Simple: Understanding God's Unfolding Promises to His People.* Phillipsburg, NJ: P&R, 2014.

Ridderbos, Herman. *The Coming of the Kingdom.* Edited by Raymond O. Zorn. Translated by H. de Jongste. Philadelphia: P&R, 1962.

Roberts, Andrew. *Churchill: Walking with Destiny.* New York: Viking, 2018.

_____. *The Storm of War: A New History of the Second World War.* New York: Harper, 2011.

Robertson, O. Palmer. *The Christ of the Covenants.* Phillipsburg, NJ: P&R, 1980.

_____. *The Christ of the Prophets.* Phillipsburg, NJ: P&R, 2004.

Schreiner, Thomas R. *Covenant and God's Purpose for the World.* SSBT. Wheaton, IL: Crossway, 2017.

_____. *Romans.* BECNT. 2nd ed. Grand Rapids, MI: Baker Academic, 2018.

Sklar, Jay. *Leviticus: An Introduction and Commentary.* TOTC 3. Downers Grove, IL: IVP Academic, 2013.

Timmins, Will N. *Romans 7 and Christian Identity: A Study of the 'I' in its Literary Context.* SNTSMS 170. Cambridge: Cambridge University Press, 2017.

Turretin, Francis. *Institutes of Elenctic Theology.* Edited by James T. Dennison Jr. Translated by George Musgrave Giger. 3 vols. Phillipsburg, NJ: P&R, 1992–97.

VanGemeren, Willem A. *Interpreting the Prophetic Word: An Introduction to the Prophetic Literature of the Old Testament.* Grand Rapids, MI: Zondervan, 1990.

Vos, Geerhardus. *Biblical Theology: Old and New Testaments.* 1948. Reprint, Edinburgh: Banner of Truth, 1975.

_____. "The Doctrine of the Covenant in Reformed Theology." In *Redemptive History and Biblical Interpretation: The Shorter Writings of Geerhardus Vos,* ed. Richard B. Gaffin Jr., 257-58. Phillipsburg, NJ: P&R, 1980.

_____. *Grace and Glory: Sermons Preached in the Chapel of Princeton Theological Seminary.* Edinburgh: Banner of Truth, 1994.

_____. "Hungering and Thirsting After Righteousness." In *Grace and Glory: Sermons Preached in the Chapel of Princeton Theological Seminary.* Edinburgh: Banner of Truth, 1994.

_____. *Redemptive History and Biblical Interpretation: The Shorter Writings of Geerhardus Vos.* Edited by Richard B. Gaffin Jr. Phillipsburg, NJ: P&R, 1980.

_____. *Reformed Dogmatics.* Translated and edited by Richard B. Gaffin Jr. 5 vols. Bellingham, WA: Lexham Press, 2012–16.

_____. "The Scriptural Doctrine of the Love of God." In *Redemptive History and Biblical Interpretation: The Shorter Writings of Geerhardus Vos,* ed. Richard B. Gaffin Jr, 430-35. Phillipsburg, NJ: P&R, 1980.

_____. *The Teaching of Jesus Concerning the Kingdom of God and the Church.* N.p. Reprint, Fontes, 2017.

Waltke, Bruce K. *The Book of Proverbs: Chapters 1–15.* NICOT. Grand Rapids, MI: Eerdmans, 2004.

Waltke, Bruce K. with Cathi J. Fredricks. *Genesis: A Commentary.* Grand Rapids, MI: Zondervan, 2002.

Waltke, Bruce K. with Charles Yu. *An Old Testament Theology: An Exegetical, Canonical, and Thematic Approach.* Grand Rapids, MI: Zondervan, 2007.

Waters, Guy Prentiss, J. Nicholas Reid, and John R. Muether, eds. *Covenant Theology: Biblical, Theological, and Historical Perspectives.* Wheaton, IL: Crossway, 2020.

Wenham, Gordon J. *Genesis 1–15.* WBC 1. Nashville: Thomas Nelson, 1987.

AUTHOR INDEX

SCRIPTURE INDEX

ESSENTIAL STUDIES IN
BIBLICAL THEOLOGY

FROM ADAM AND ISRAEL
TO THE CHURCH
A Biblical Theology
of the People of God

BENJAMIN L. GLADD

EXODUS
OLD AND NEW
A Biblical Theology
of Redemption

L. MICHAEL MORALES

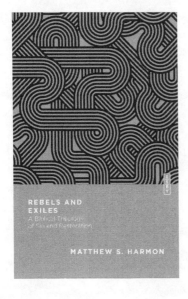

REBELS AND
EXILES
A Biblical Theology
of Sin and Restoration

MATTHEW S. HARMON

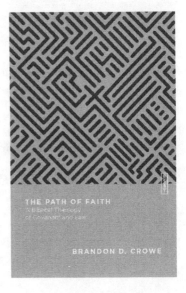

THE PATH OF FAITH
A Biblical Theology
of Covenant and Law

BRANDON D. CROWE